Pages in the Science Section Introduce Concepts:

- Living and Nonliving Things
- Plants and Animals Grow and Change
- Plants and Animals Have Basic Needs
- Our Bodies Need Good Care
- Our Five Senses Help Us Observe the World Around Us
- Earth Changes
- Forces Around Us

Pages in the Social Studies Section Introduce Concepts:

- Positional Words
- Families Are Different
- Families Observe Traditions and Celebrations
- People Have Basic Needs
- People Have Jobs
- People Work and Live in Communities
- Money Buys Things
- Maps Show Places
- Citizens Follow Rules
- Transportation Helps People
- Technology Gives Information
- People Used Different Tools in the Past

Stages of Development

STAGES OF DEVELOPMENT OF THREE- AND FOUR-YEAR-OLDS

The intellectual development of four-year-olds is expanding rapidly. These children are able to understand more abstract skills and eagerly accept new challenges. Their language and math skills begin to increase greatly. Five-year-olds are beginning to recognize their relationship to their families and the world. They enjoy sharing experiences with others and can give and receive feedback. Because each child is unique and learns at his or her own pace, it is important for parents to follow their child's lead in determining when to introduce various skills.

A four-year-old:
- speaks in fairly complex sentences
- listens attentively to stories for 10 to 15 minutes
- enjoys singing simple songs, rhymes, and nonsense words
- tells simple stories from pictures or books
- asks and answers *who, what, when, why,* and *where* questions
- recognizes many letters, if taught
- understands that letters make sounds
- prints own name, if taught
- recognizes familiar words in simple books or signs
- identifies common colors and shapes
- recognizes most numbers to 10
- counts 8 to 10 objects
- understands concepts up to 8
- understands basic concepts related to attributes
- solves simple, concrete problems
- follows 2 unrelated directions

A five-year-old:
- speaks in complex sentences
- listens to, responds to, and discusses stories
- begins to develop appropriate questions in response to discussions
- shares personal narratives through show and tell
- recognizes many letters and the sounds they make
- connects the written word with personal experience
- begins to recognize organizational features of printed text
- reads, writes, compares, counts, and orders numbers up to 10
- recognizes numbers to 20
- compares and orders objects to some attribute, such as shortest to tallest or biggest to littlest
- identifies basic shapes in the world around him or her
- explores the world using his or her senses
- observes, compares, and describes things he or she sees
- draws pictures to communicate observations

The standards listed are tools that serve as benchmarks of a child's development. It is important to keep in mind that young children develop at different rates. Some children will be taking the first steps toward understanding the concepts, while others will be mastering them. The standards can be used with your child to guide practice and to measure progress.

Language Arts

Recognizes and names some letters
Understands that letters make sounds
Uses a pencil or crayons effectively
Names basic colors
Recognizes rhyming words
Retells information

Math

Uses positional terms to describe relationships among objects
Sorts and classifies objects by one attribute
Begins to draw and recognize basic geometric shapes
Begins to recognize a penny, nickel, dime, and quarter
Recognizes and names numbers to 10
Understands concepts of *more than*, *less than*, and *equal to*
Counts objects using one-to-one correspondence
Demonstrates a beginning understanding of measurement
Makes comparisons using the terms *same* and *different*
Recognizes and extends patterns

Science

Understands the difference in living and nonliving things
Understands the variety of living things
Begins to understand how living things function, adapt, and change
Uses senses to explore and observe materials
Names major body parts
Makes comparisons among objects that have been observed
Describes basic needs of living things, such as air and water
Names things that are from Earth, such as water, food, and soil
Identifies ways that people can take care of Earth
Recognizes that Earth changes
Begins to understand characteristics of matter

Social Studies

Understands that humans have basic needs
Identifies differences among people and families
Recognizes customs and traditions of families
Recognizes customs and national symbols of his or her country
Understands the concept of location and uses terms to express it
Recognizes parts of a community
Identifies jobs that people do
Explains why people have jobs
Identifies rules and their purpose
Identifies characteristics of a good citizen
Identifies examples of technology and how they meet needs
Understands different kinds of transportation
Recognizes the differences in past and present

A Tree Home

Directions: Have your child use a pencil or crayon to trace the lines from left to right to help each bird fly to its nest. Then have your child trace the lines from top to bottom to draw the tree trunk. Invite your child to color the picture.

Left to Right and Top to Bottom
3-2-1 Learn, SV 9781419099281

Flower Fun

Directions: Have your child use a pencil or crayon to trace the lines of the circles in the flower. Then have your child trace the diagonal lines of the leaves. Invite your child to color the picture.

Diagonal Lines and Circles
3-2-1 Learn, SV 9781419099281

Picnic in the Park

Directions: Have your child use a pencil or crayon to draw a line *above* each animal. Then have your child write an **X** *below* each food. Invite your child to color the picture.

Above and Below
3-2-1 Learn, SV 9781419099281

Swim Time

Directions: Have your child use a pencil or crayon to circle the frog that is *on* the lily pad and draw a line above the frog that is *off* the lily pad. Then have your child draw a box around the duck that is *out* of the water and write an **X** above the duck that is *in* the water. Invite your child to color the picture.

On, Off, In, and Out
3-2-1 Learn, SV 9781419099281

M Is for Monkey

Directions: Ask your child to name the animal and listen for the beginning sound. Read the sentence aloud and invite your child to say the words that begin like the picture name. Then ask your child to use a pencil or crayon to add a mop to the big picture to match the sentence. Next have your child color the three pictures that begin with the *m* sound. Finally have your child trace the letters.

The **monkey** has a **mop**.

Letter *Mm*
3-2-1 Learn, SV 9781419099281

D Is for Dog

Directions: Ask your child to name the animal and listen for the beginning sound. Read the sentence aloud and invite your child to say the words that begin like the picture name. Then ask your child to use a pencil or crayon to add a dish to the big picture to match the sentence. Next have your child color the three pictures that begin with the *d* sound. Finally have your child trace the letters.

The **dog** eats from a **dish**.

F Is for Fox

Directions: Ask your child to name the animal and listen for the beginning sound. Read the sentence aloud and invite your child to say the words that begin like the picture name. Then ask your child to use a pencil or crayon to add a fork to the big picture to match the sentence. Next have your child color the three pictures that begin with the *f* sound. Finally have your child trace the letters.

The **fox** eats with a **fork**.

3-2-1 Learn, SV 9781419099281

G Is for Goat

Directions: Ask your child to name the animal and listen for the beginning sound. Read the sentence and invite your child to say the words that begin like the picture name. Then ask your child to use a pencil or crayon to add a game to the big picture to match the sentence. Next have your child color the three pictures that begin with the *g* sound. Finally have your child trace the letters.

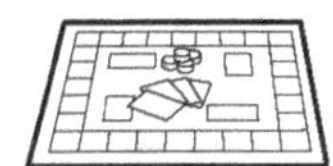

The **goat** plays a **game**.

G G g g

Letter Gg
3-2-1 Learn, SV 9781419099281

B Is for Bus

Directions: Ask your child to name the object and listen for the beginning sound. Read the sentence and invite your child to say the words that begin like the picture name. Then ask your child to use a pencil or crayon to add a bird to the big picture to match the sentence. Next have your child color the three pictures that begin with the *b* sound. Finally have your child trace the letters.

A **bird** is on the **bus**.

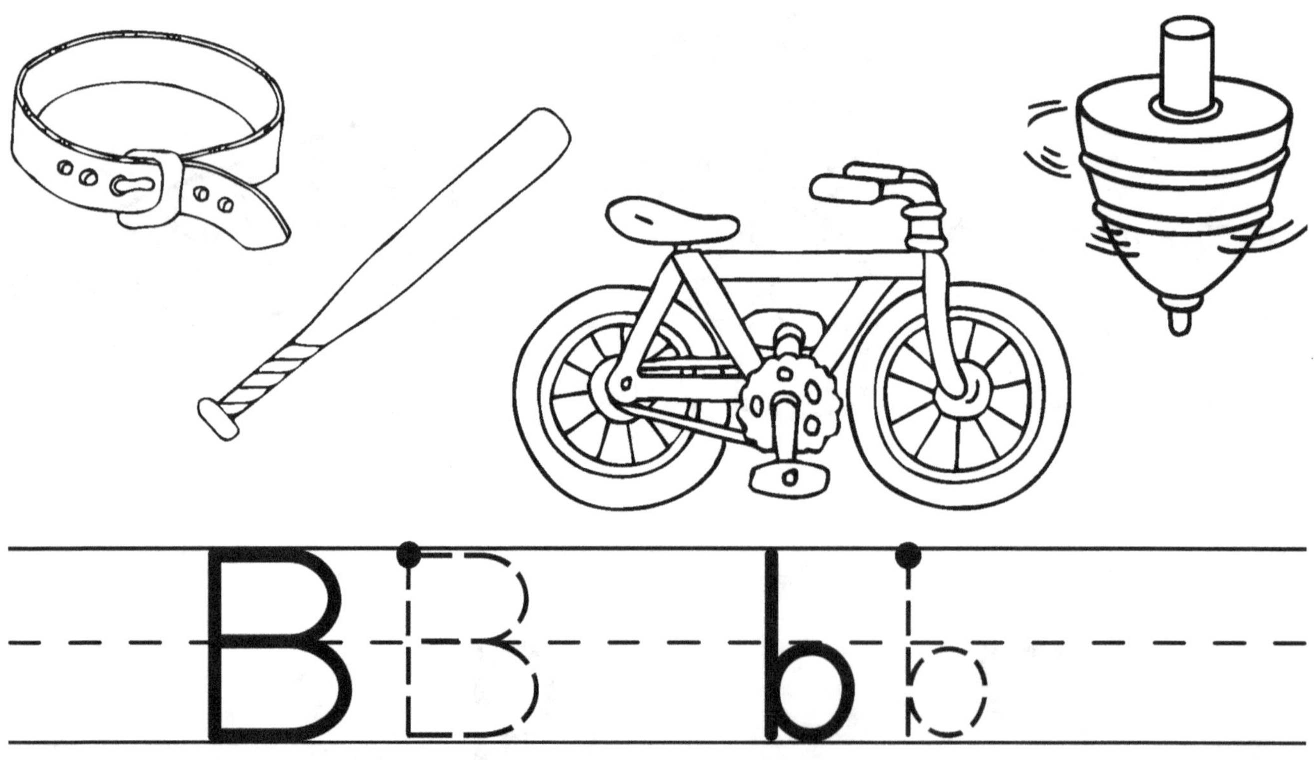

T Is for Turtle

Directions: Ask your child to name the animal and listen for the beginning sound. Read the sentence and invite your child to say the words that begin like the picture name. Then ask your child to use a pencil or crayon to add a telephone to the big picture to match the sentence. Next have your child color the three pictures that begin with the *t* sound. Finally have your child trace the letters.

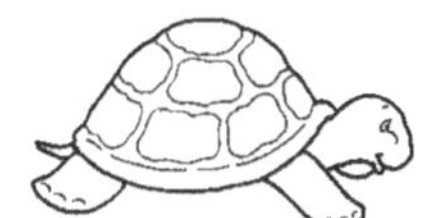 

The **turtle** talks on the **telephone**.

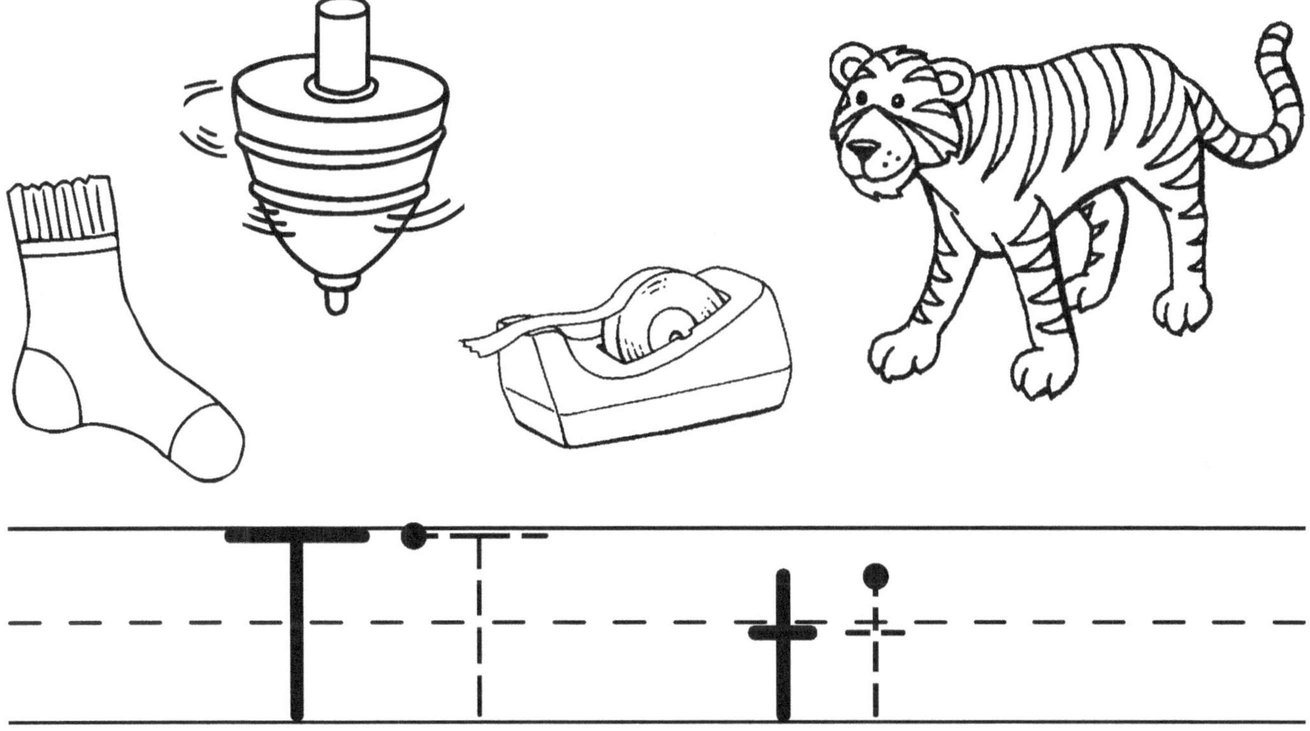

Letter *Tt*
3-2-1 Learn, SV 9781419099281

S Is for Seal

Directions: Ask your child to name the animal and listen for the beginning sound. Read the sentence and invite your child to say the words that begin like the picture name. Then ask your child to use a pencil or crayon to add a sun to the big picture to match the sentence. Next have your child color the three pictures that begin with the *s* sound. Finally have your child trace the letters.

The **seal** sits under the **sun**.

Letter Ss
3-2-1 Learn, SV 9781419099281

W Is for Wagon

Directions: Ask your child to name the object and listen for the beginning sound. Read the sentence and invite your child to say the words that begin like the picture name. Then ask your child to use a pencil or crayon to add a worm to the big picture to match the sentence. Next have your child color the three pictures that begin with the *w* sound. Finally have your child trace the letters.

The **worm** is in the **wagon**.

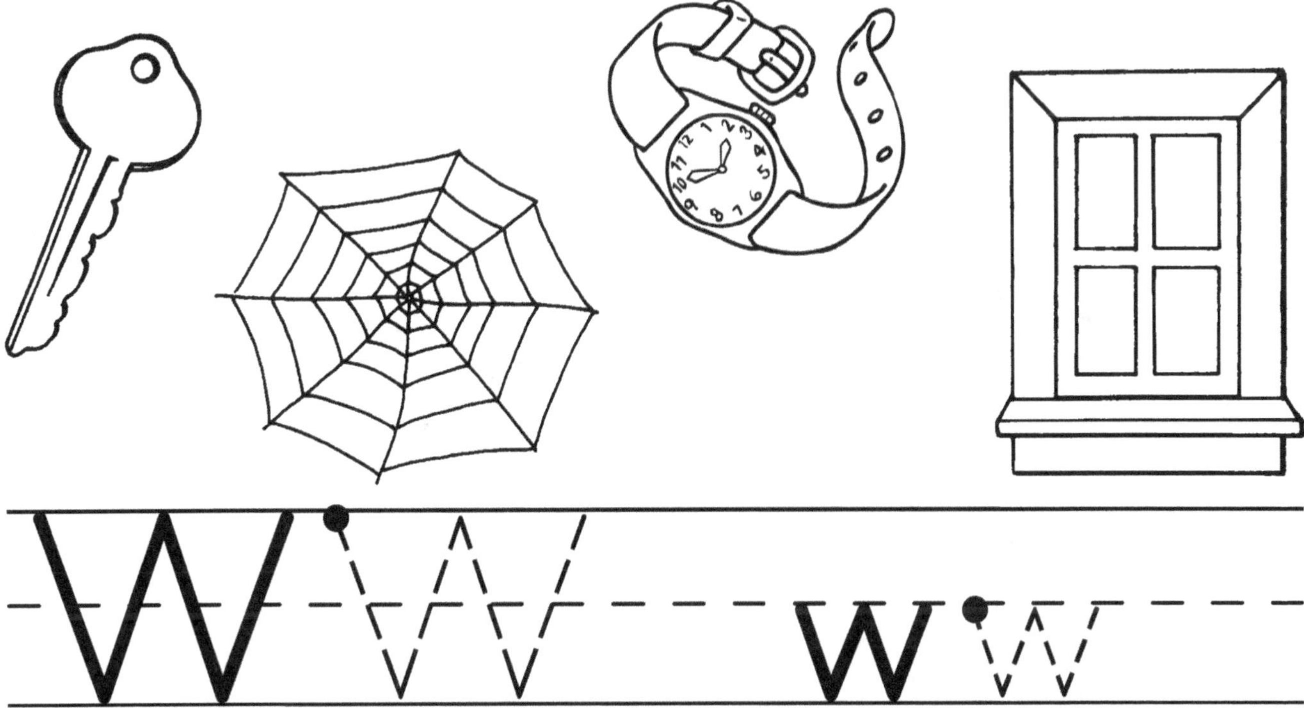

Letter Ww
3-2-1 Learn, SV 9781419099281

K Is for Kangaroo

Directions: Ask your child to name the animal and listen for the beginning sound. Read the sentence and invite your child to say the words that begin like the picture name. Then ask your child to use a pencil or crayon to add a kite to the big picture to match the sentence. Next have your child color the three pictures that begin with the *k* sound. Finally have your child trace the letters.

The **kangaraoo** flies a **kite**.

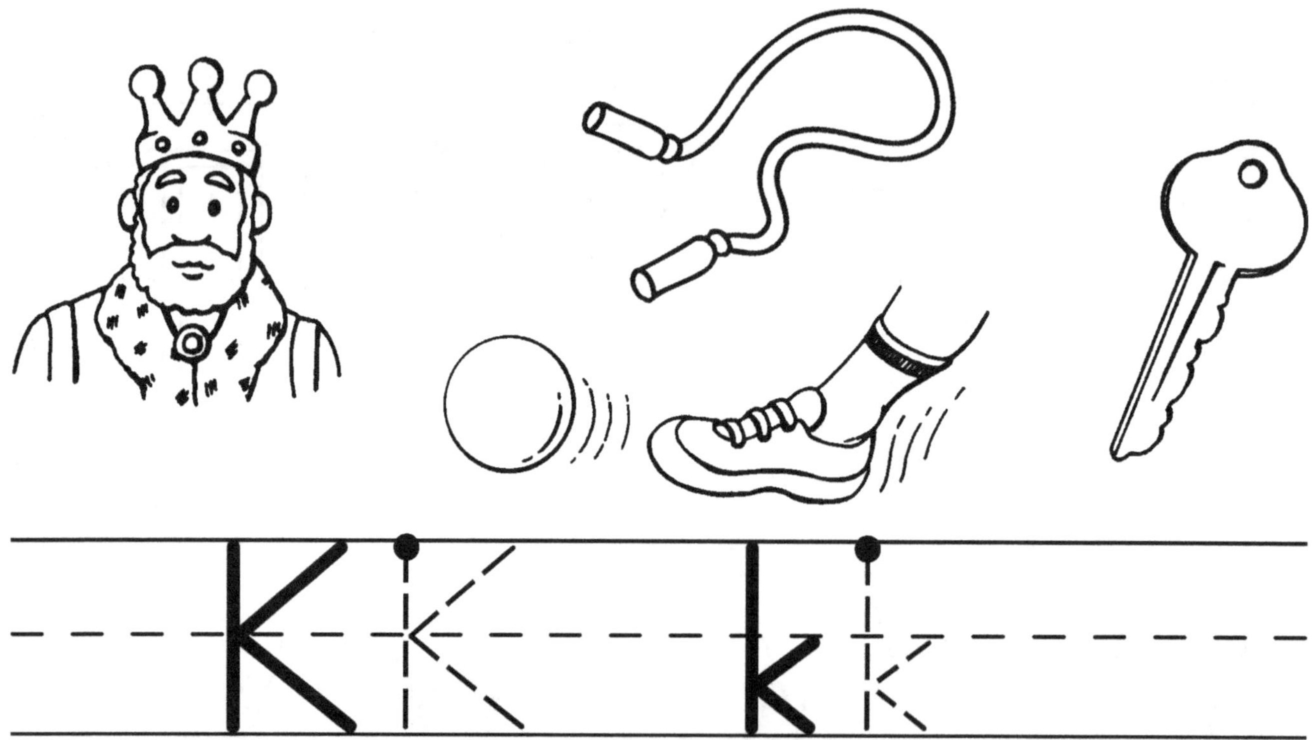

Letter Kk
3-2-1 Learn, SV 9781419099281

J Is for Jar

Directions: Ask your child to name the object and listen for the beginning sound. Read the sentence and invite your child to say the words that begin like the picture name. Then ask your child to use a pencil or crayon to add jam to the big picture to match the sentence. Next have your child color the three pictures that begin with the *j* sound. Finally have your child trace the letters.

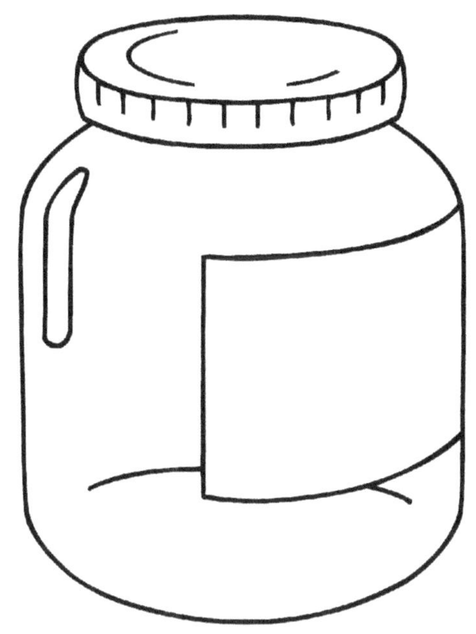

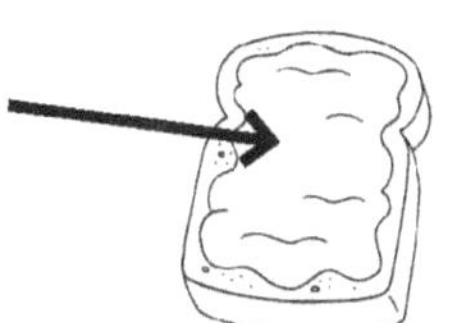

The **jam** is in the **jar**.

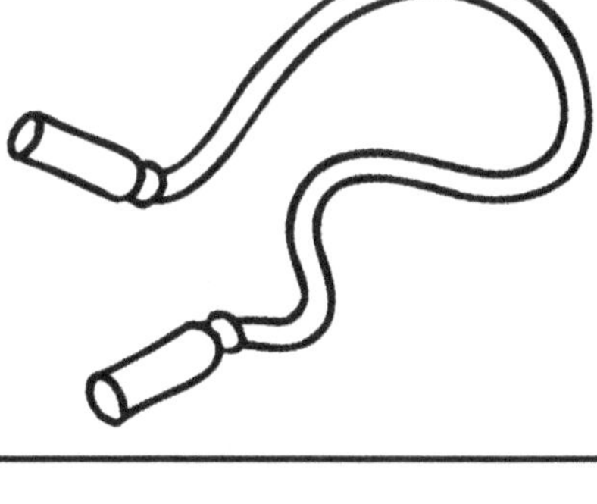

3-2-1 Learn, SV 9781419099281

P Is for Peach

Directions: Ask your child to name the object and listen for the beginning sound. Read the sentence and invite your child to say the words that begin like the picture name. Then ask your child to use a pencil or crayon to add a plate to the big picture to match the sentence. Next have your child color the three pictures that begin with the *p* sound. Finally have your child trace the letters.

 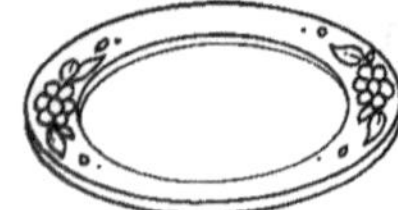

The **peach** is on the **plate**.

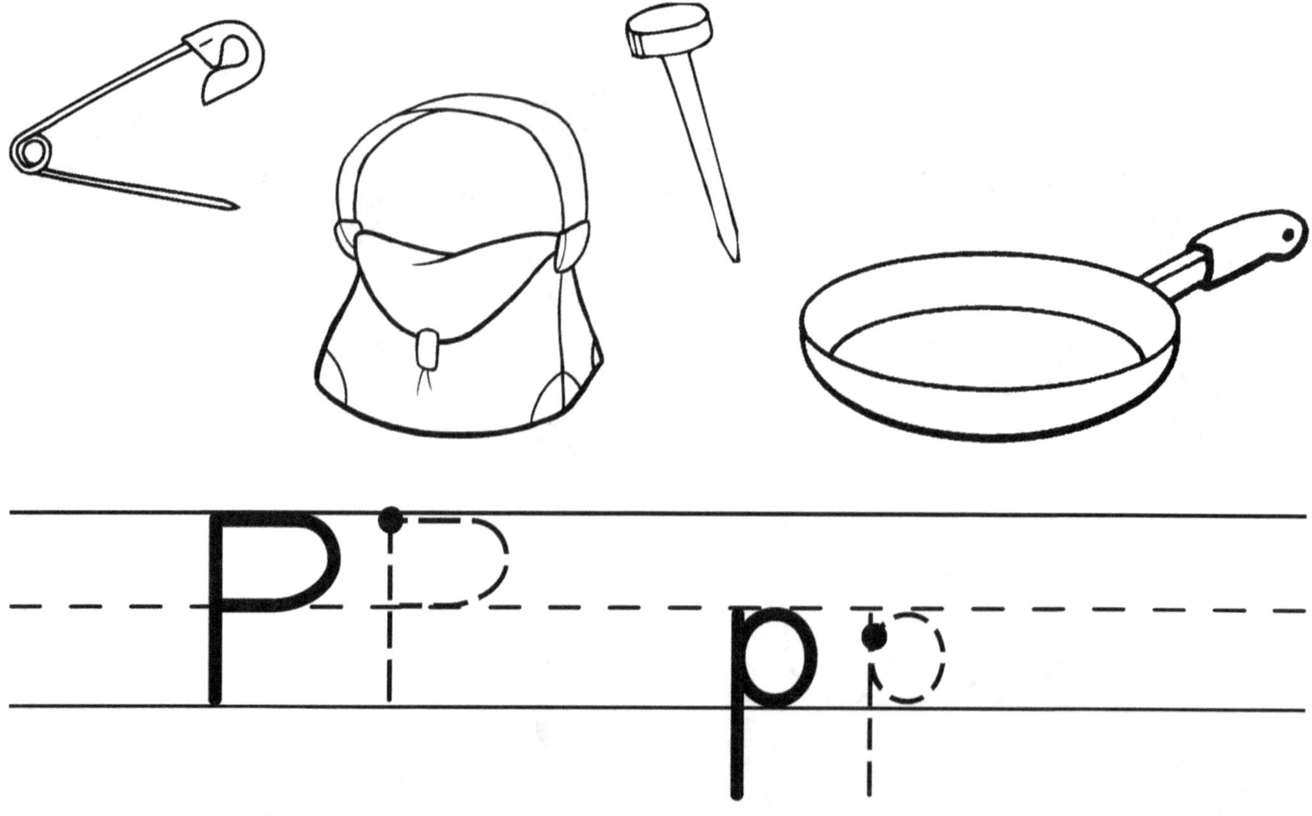

20

N Is for Nurse

Directions: Ask your child to name the person and listen for the beginning sound. Read the sentence and invite your child to say the words that begin like the picture name. Then ask your child to use a pencil or crayon to add a nest to the big picture to match the sentence. Next have your child color the three pictures that begin with the *n* sound. Finally have your child trace the letters.

The **nurse** sees a **nest**.

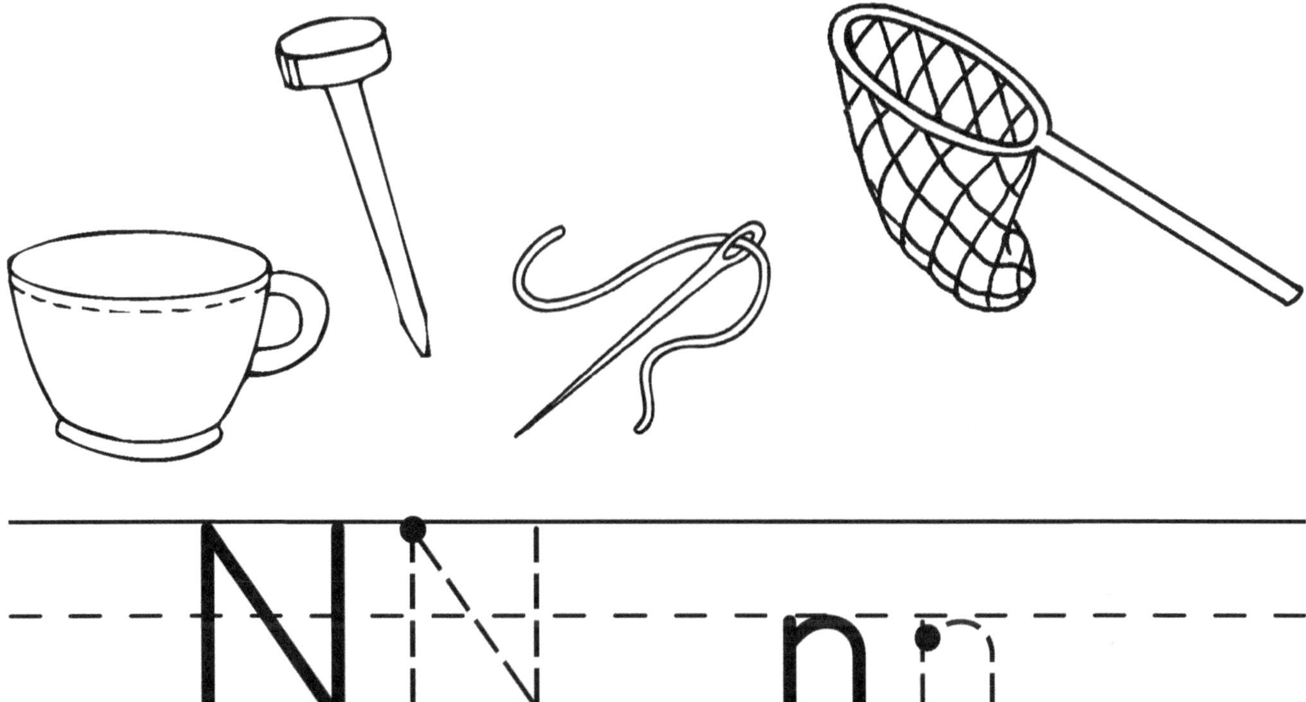

Letter Nn
3-2-1 Learn, SV 9781419099281

C Is for Car

Directions: Ask your child to name the object and listen for the beginning sound. Read the sentence and invite your child to say the words that begin like the picture name. Then ask your child to use a pencil or crayon to add a cat to the big picture to match the sentence. Next have your child color the three pictures that begin with the *c* sound. Finally have your child trace the letters.

The **cat** is in the **car**.

Letter Cc
3-2-1 Learn, SV 9781419099281

H Is for Horse

Directions: Ask your child to name the animal and listen for the beginning sound. Read the sentence and invite your child to say the words that begin like the picture name. Then ask your child to use a pencil or crayon to add a hat to the big picture to match the sentence. Next have your child color the three pictures that begin with the *h* sound. Finally have your child trace the letters.

The **hat** is on the **horse**.

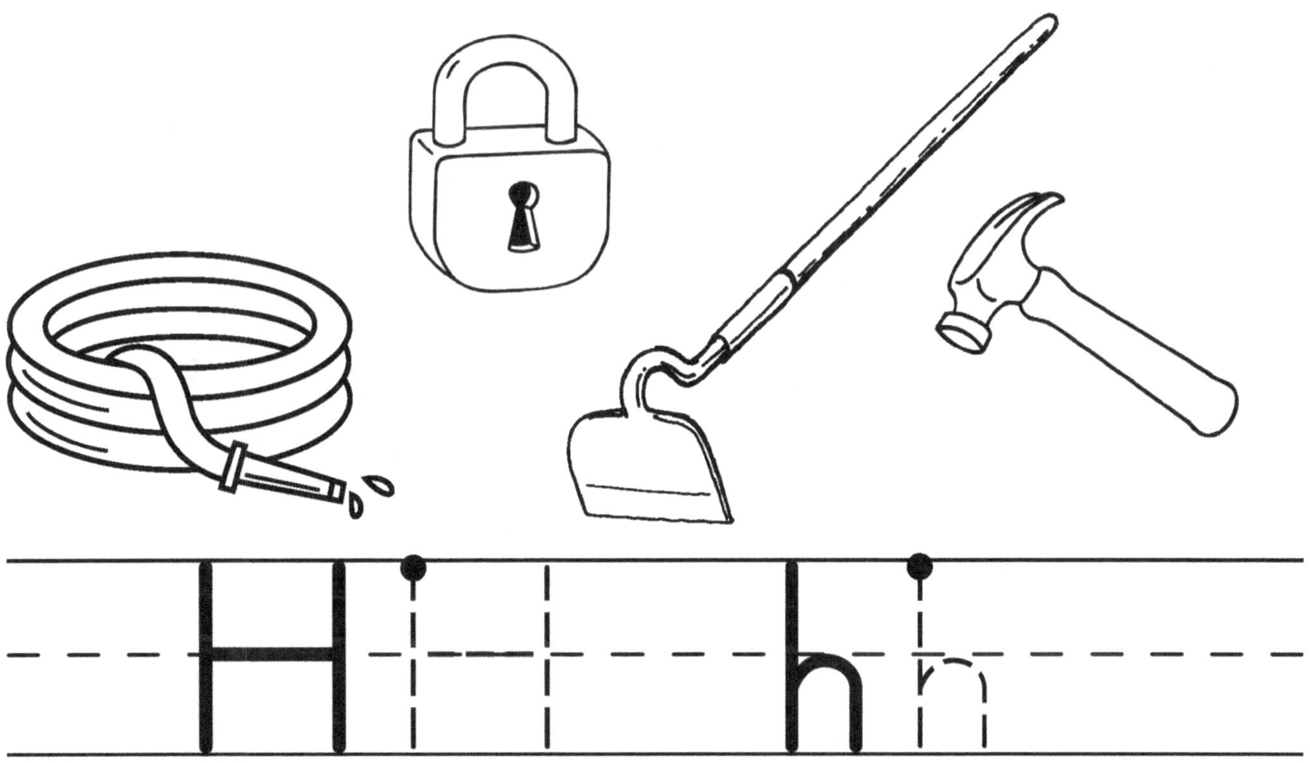

Letter Hh
3-2-1 Learn, SV 9781419099281

L Is for Lion

Directions: Ask your child to name the animal and listen for the beginning sound. Read the sentence and invite your child to say the words that begin like the picture name. Then ask your child to use a pencil or crayon to add a log to the big picture to match the sentence. Next have your child color the three pictures that begin with the *l* sound. Finally have your child trace the letters.

The **lion** is on the **log**.

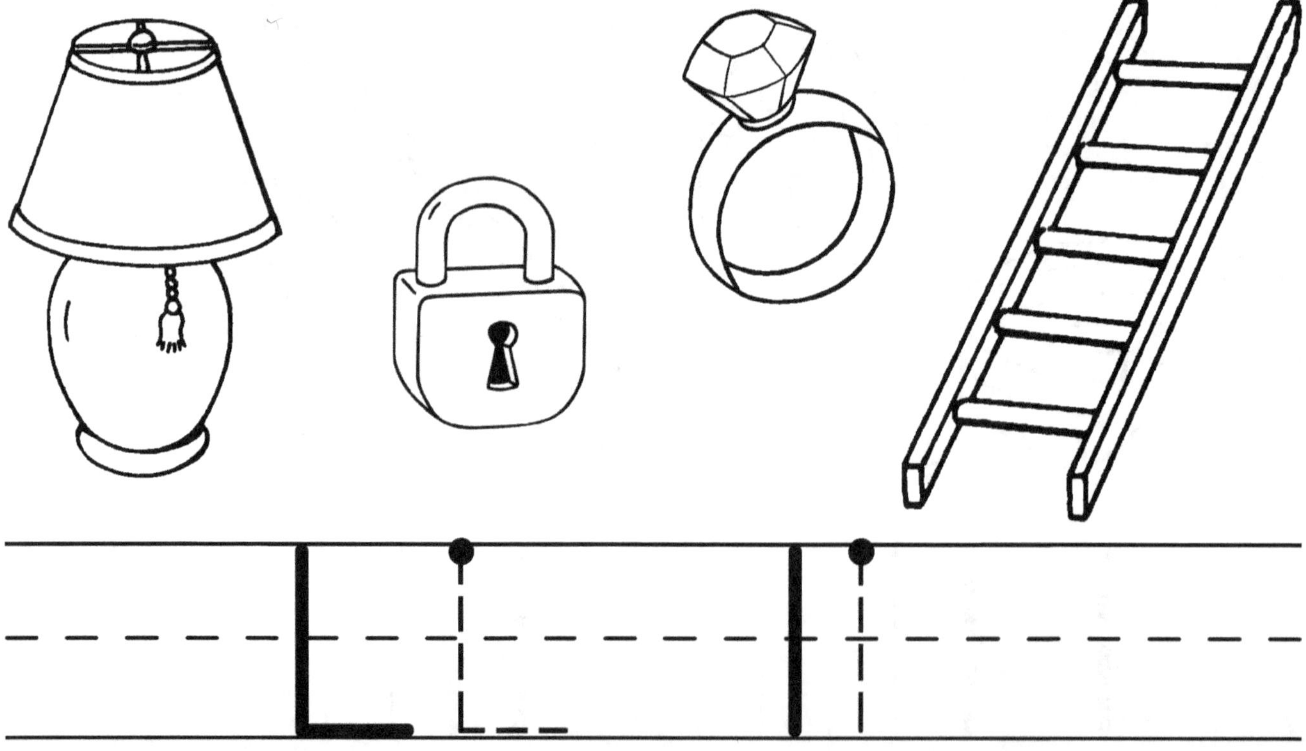

R Is for Rabbit

Directions: Ask your child to name the animal and listen for the beginning sound. Read the sentence and invite your child to say the words that begin like the picture name. Then ask your child to use a pencil or crayon to add a rainbow to the big picture to match the sentence. Next have your child color the three pictures that begin with the *r* sound. Finally have your child trace the letters.

The **rabbit** is below the **rainbow**.

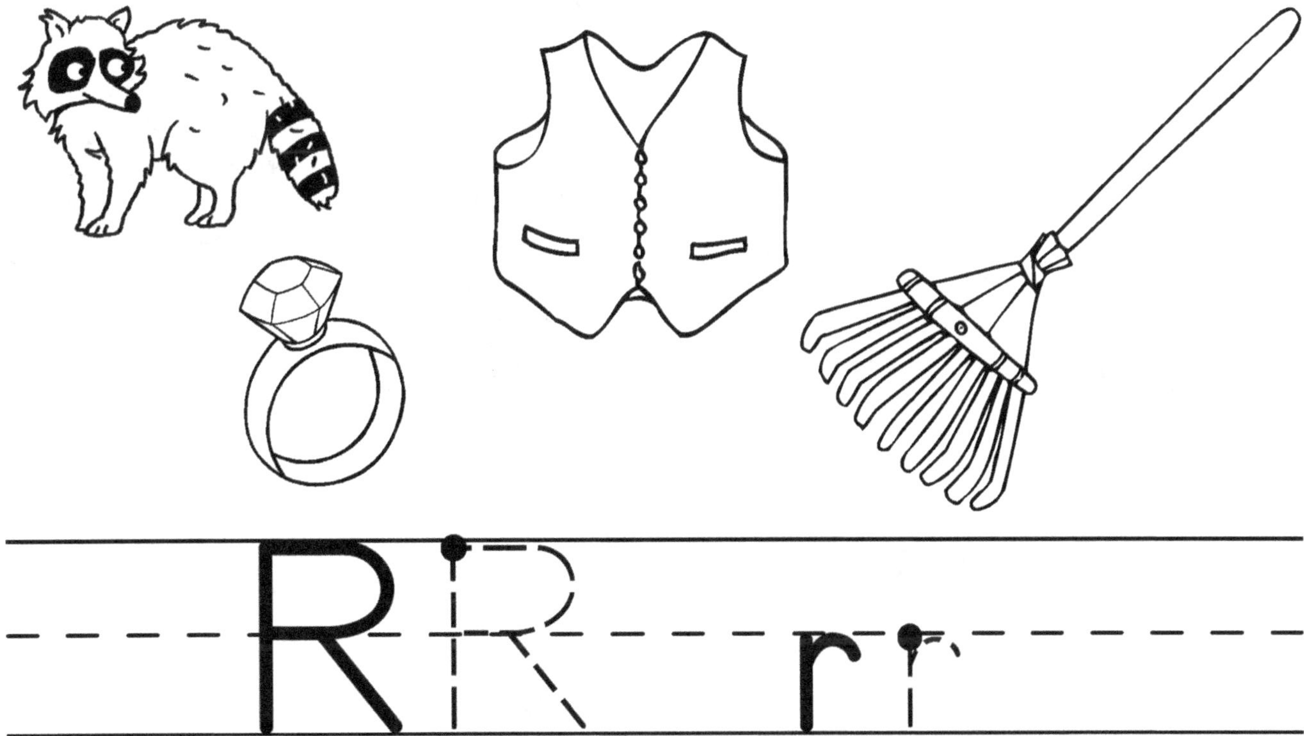

3-2-1 Learn, SV 9781419099281

V Is for Van

Directions: Ask your child to name the object and listen for the beginning sound. Read the sentence and invite your child to say the words that begin like the picture name. Then ask your child to use a pencil or crayon to add vegetables to the big picture to match the sentence. Next have your child color the three pictures that begin with the *v* sound. Finally have your child trace the letters.

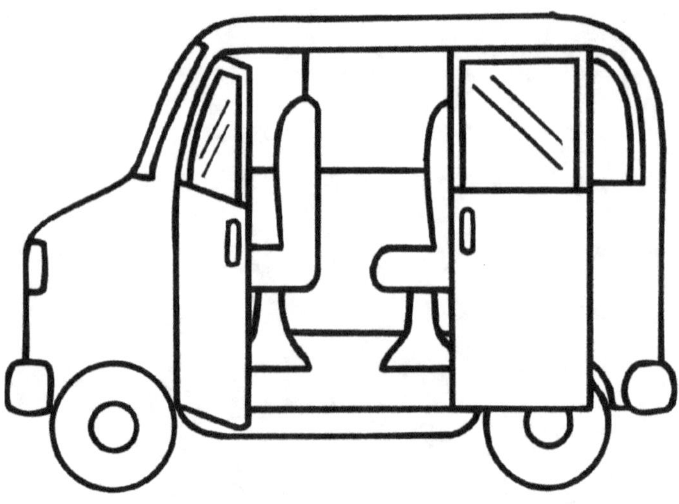

The **vegetables** are in the **van.**

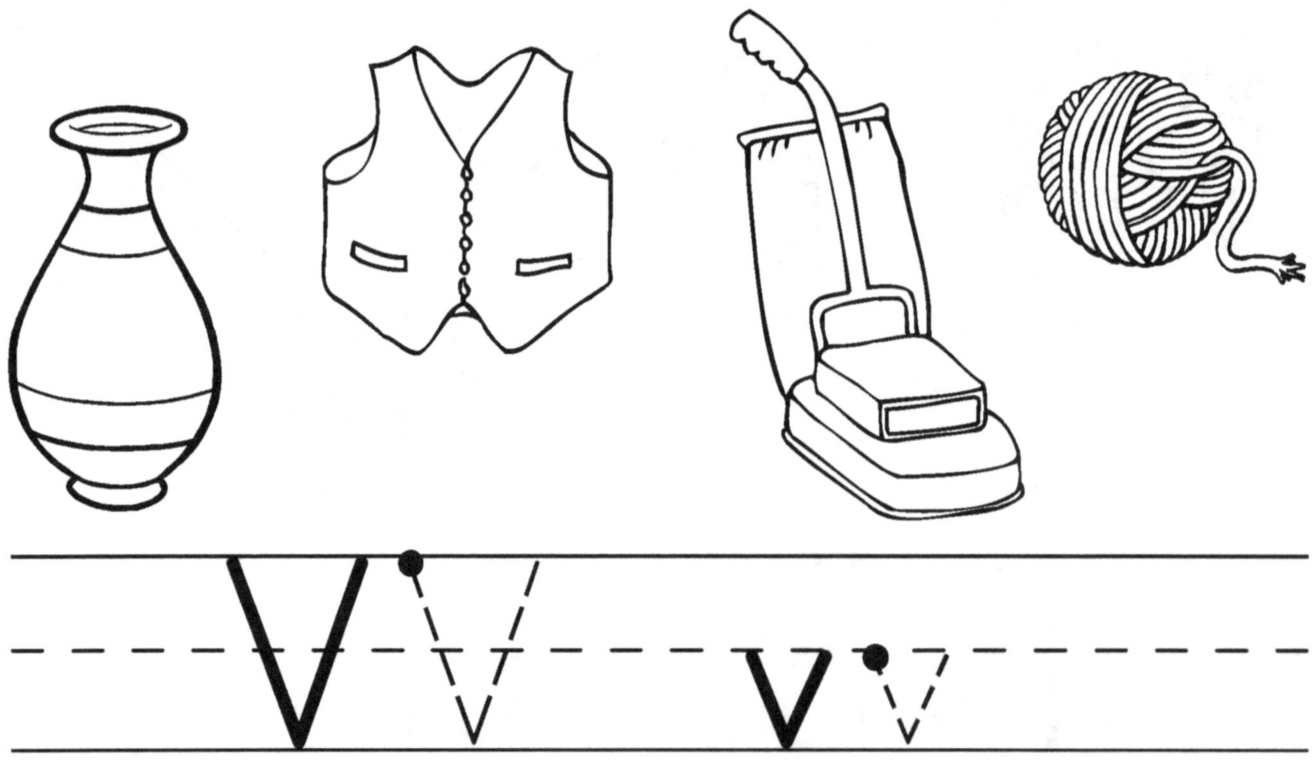

Letter Vv
3-2-1 Learn, SV 9781419099281

Y Is for Yak

The **yak** has a **yo-yo**.

Letter Yy

3-2-1 Learn, SV 9781419099281

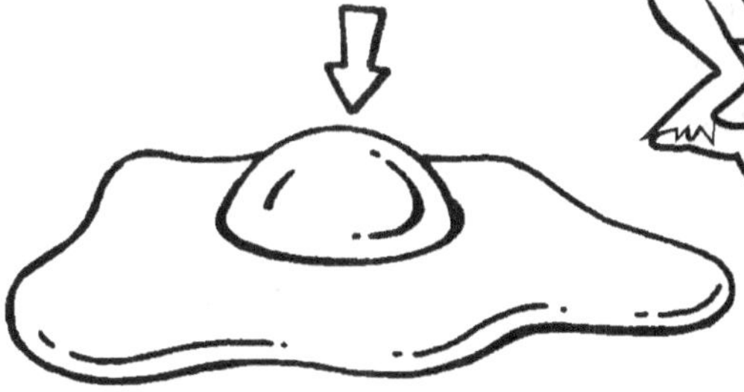

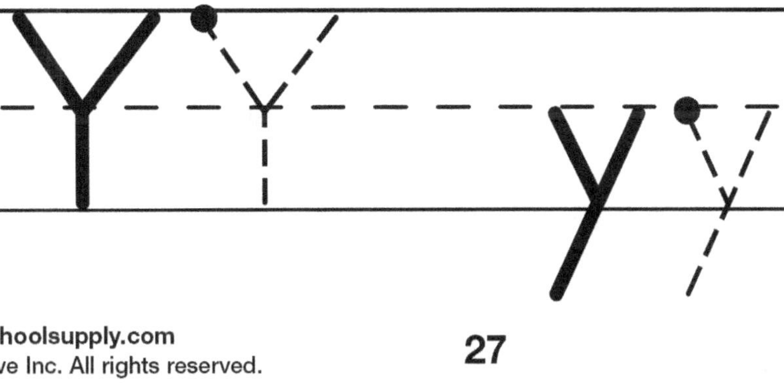

Z Is for Zoo

Directions: Ask your child to name the place and listen for the beginning sound. Read the sentence and invite your child to say the words that begin like the picture name. Then ask your child to use a pencil or crayon to add a zebra to the big picture to match the sentence. Next have your child color the three pictures that begin with the *z* sound. Finally have your child trace the letters.

The **zebra** is in the **zoo**.

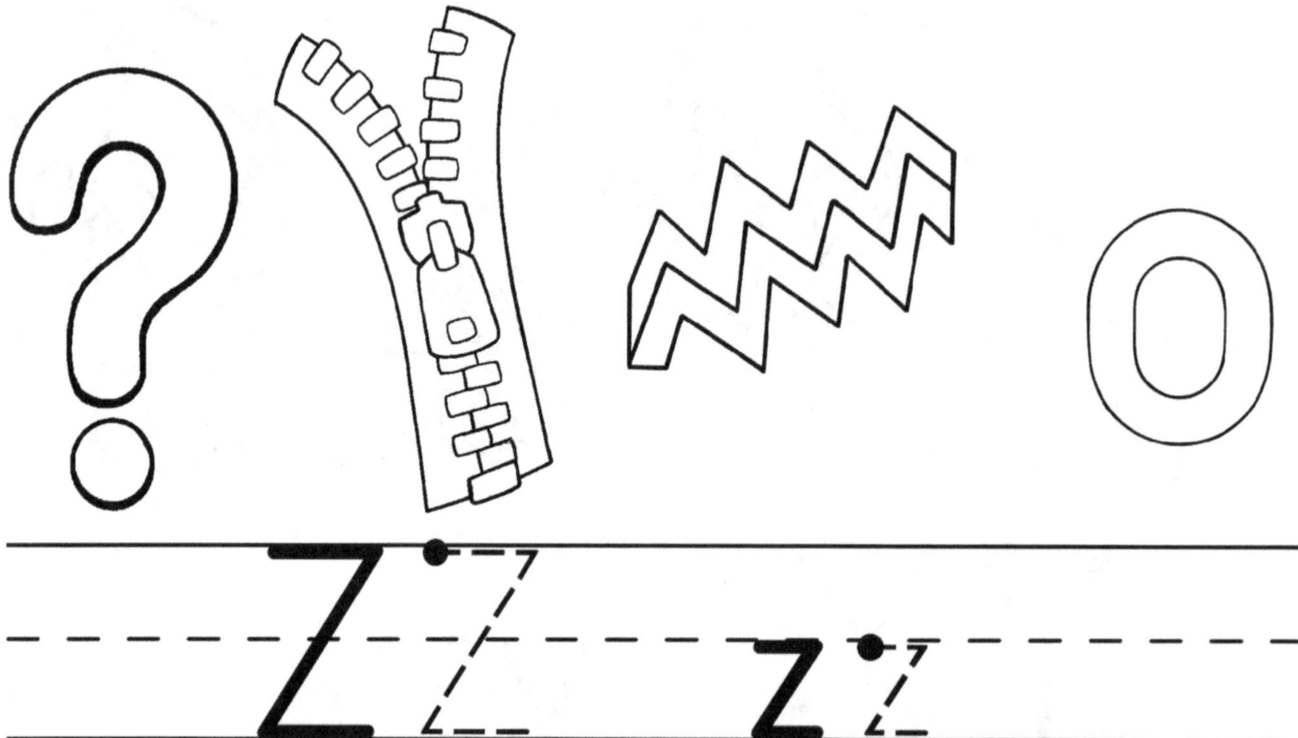

www.harcourtschoolsupply.com
© Harcourt Achieve Inc. All rights reserved.

Letter Zz
3-2-1 Learn, SV 9781419099281

Q Is for Quail

 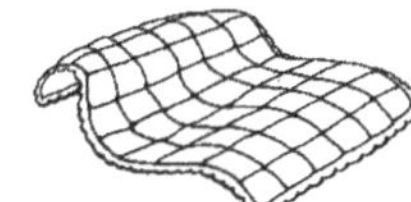

The **quail** is on the **quilt**.

X Is for Box

Directions: Ask your child to name the object and listen for the ending sound. Read the sentence and invite your child to say the words that end like the picture name. Then ask your child to use a pencil or crayon to add a fox to the big picture to match the sentence. Next have your child color the three pictures that end with the *x* sound. Finally have your child trace the letters.

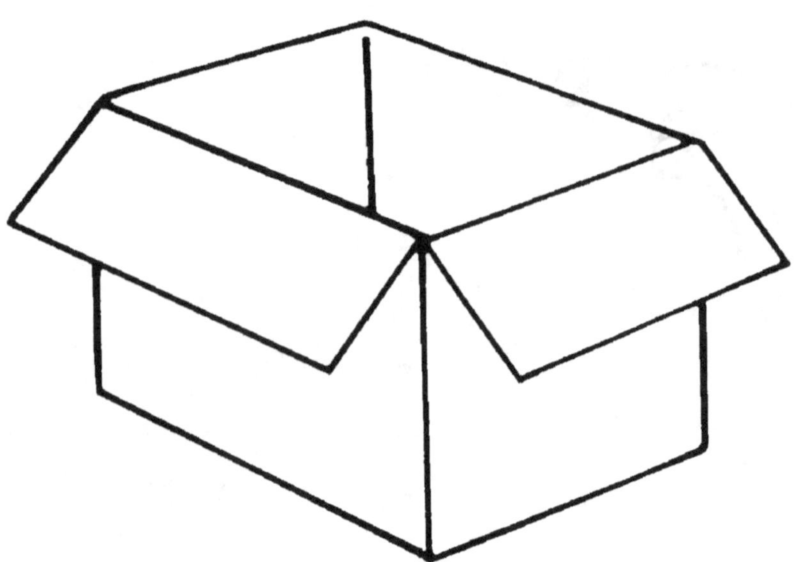

 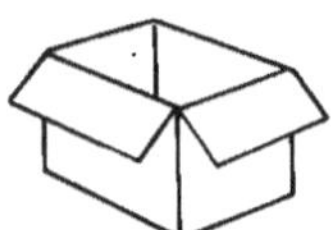

The **fox** is in the **box**.

Letter *Xx*
3-2-1 Learn, SV 9781419099281

A Is for Ant

The **ant** is on top of the **apple**.

Letter *Aa*

3-2-1 Learn, SV 9781419099281

O Is for Octopus

Directions: Ask your child to name the animal and listen for the beginning sound. Read the sentence and invite your child to say the words that begin like the picture name. Then ask your child to use a pencil or crayon to add an olive to the big picture to match the sentence. Next have your child color the three pictures that begin with the *short o* sound. Finally have your child trace the letters.

The **octopus** has an **olive**.

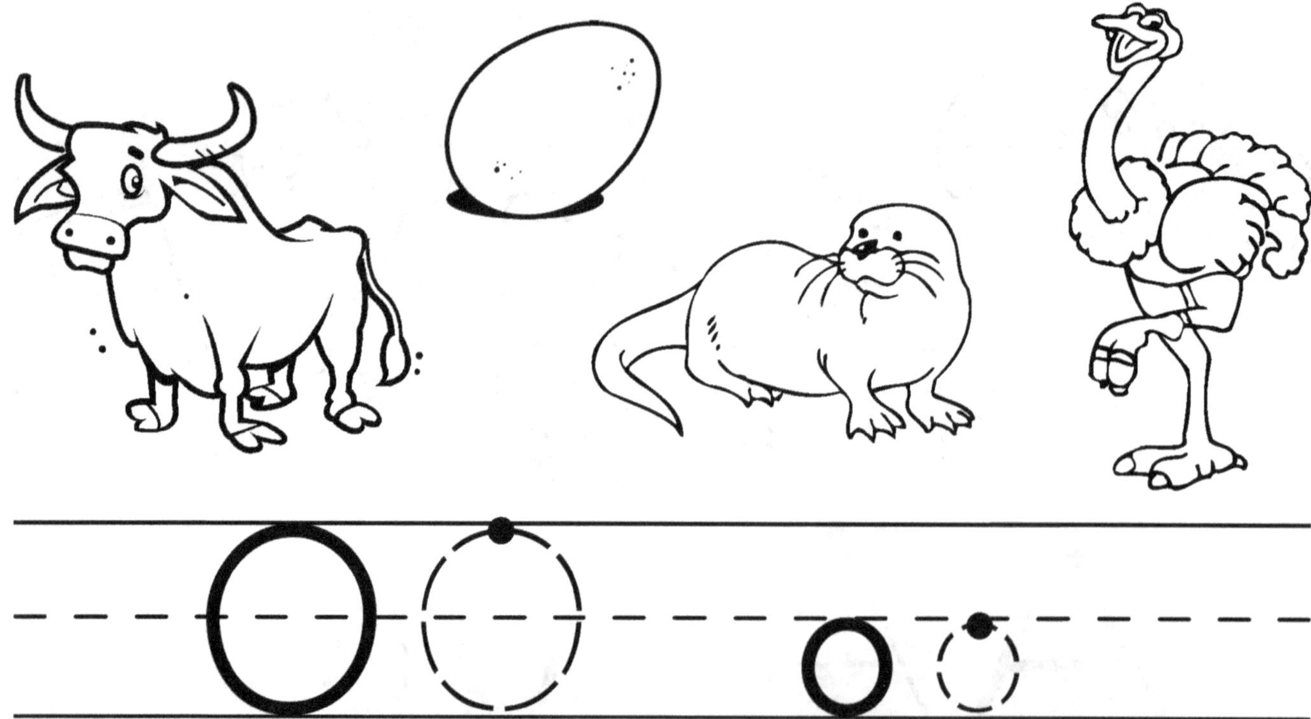

I Is for Igloo

Directions: Ask your child to name the object and listen for the beginning sound. Read the sentence and invite your child to say the words that begin like the picture name. Then ask your child to use a pencil or crayon to add an insect to the big picture to match the sentence. Next have your child color the three pictures that begin with the *short i* sound. Finally have your child trace the letters.

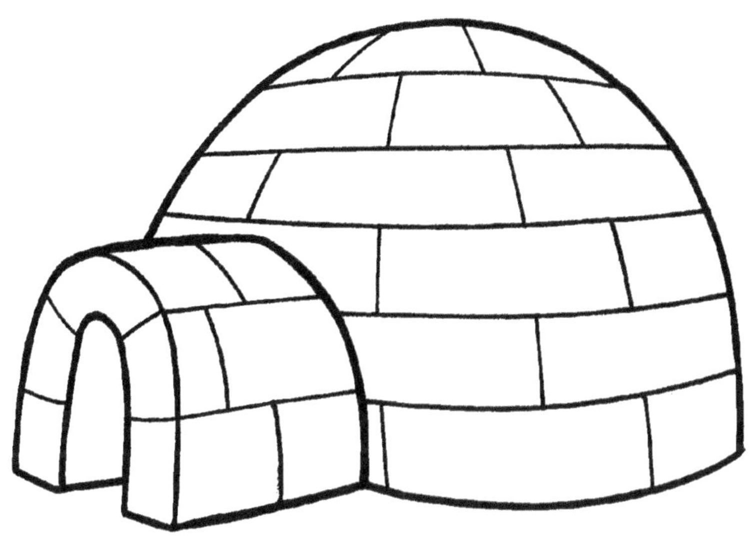

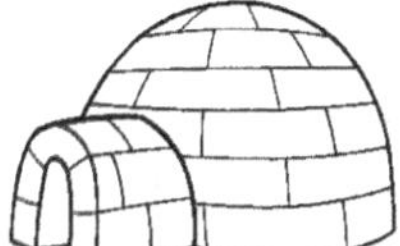

The **insect** is in the **igloo**.

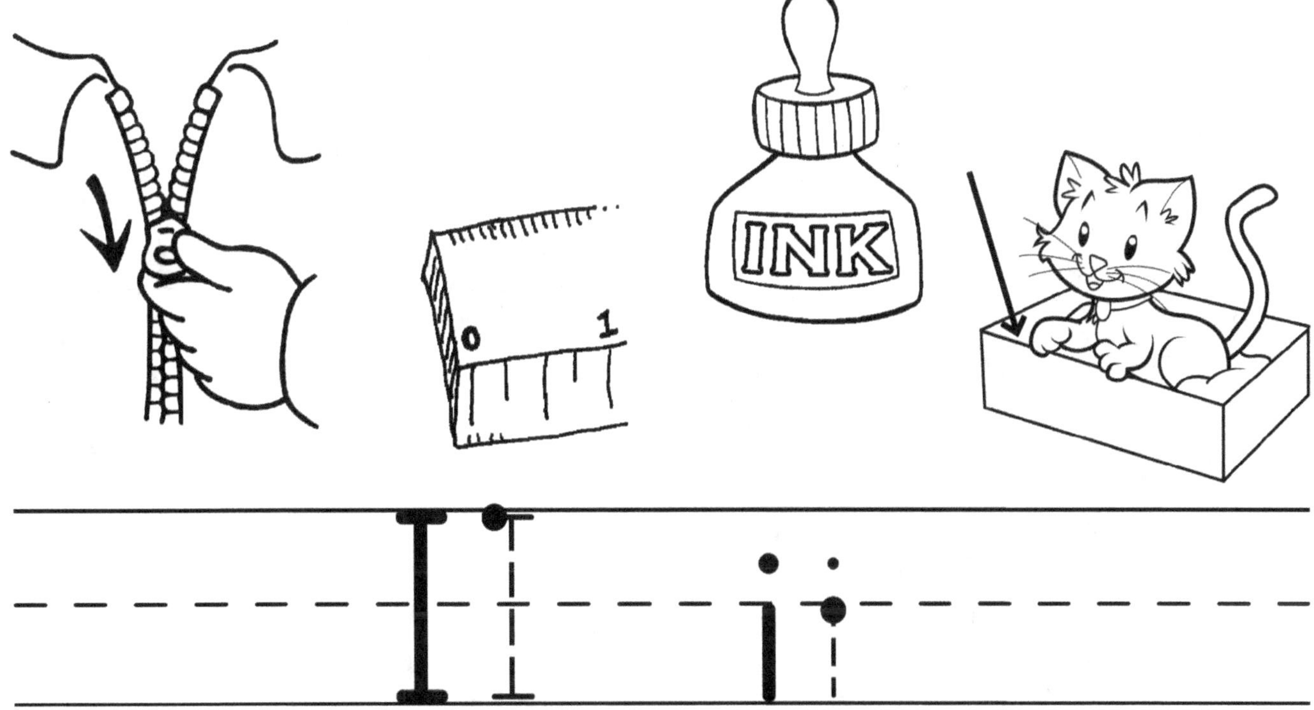

Letter *Ii*
3-2-1 Learn, SV 9781419099281

U Is for Umpire

Directions: Ask your child to name the person and listen for the beginning sound. Read the sentence and invite your child to say the words that begin like the picture name. Then ask your child to use a pencil or crayon to add an umbrella to the big picture to match the sentence. Next have your child color the three pictures that begin with the *short u* sound. Finally have your child trace the letters.

The **umpire** is under the **umbrella**.

Letter *Uu*
3-2-1 Learn, SV 9781419099281

E Is for Elephant

Directions: Ask your child to name the animal and listen for the beginning sound. Read the sentence and invite your child to say the words that begin like the picture name. Then ask your child to use a pencil or crayon to add an egg to the big picture to match the sentence. Next have your child color the three pictures that being with the *short e* sound. Finally have your child trace the letters.

The **elephant** has an **egg**.

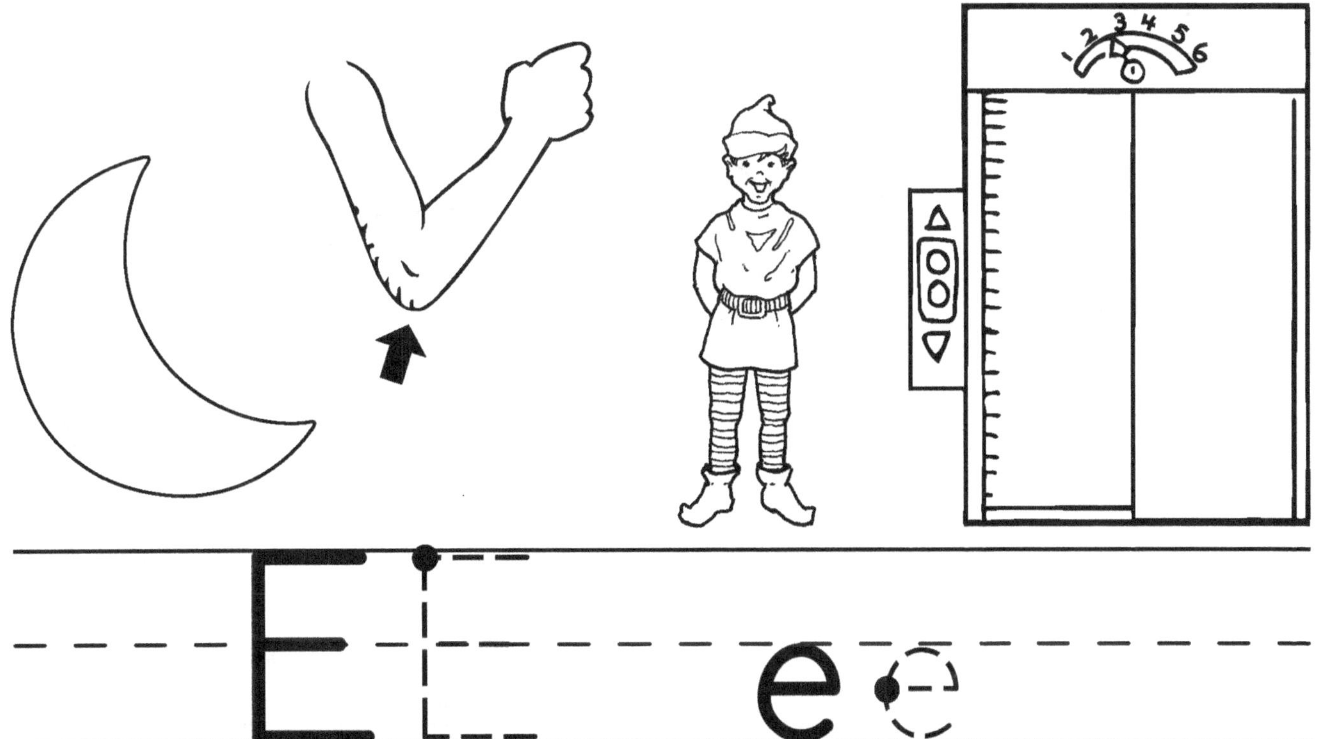

Balls of Fun

Directions: Write several pairs of partner letters, such as *Aa*, *Hh*, and *Ll*. Invite your child to identify the capital and lowercase letter in each pair. Then ask your child to color the balls that have the matching capital and lowercase letters.

Bb   Ec   Il

Pp   Rk   Mm

Zz   Hn   Dd

Partner Letters
3-2-1 Learn, SV 9781419099281

The Alphabet Maze

Directions: Write the lowercase letters of the alphabet in order and invite your child to say them. Then have your child lead the squirrel to the nut by drawing a line to show the correct alphabet order.

Alphabet Order
3-2-1 Learn, SV 9781419099281

Animal Sounds

Directions: Have your child say each animal name and listen for the beginning sound. Then ask your child to use a pencil or crayon to circle another object in each picture that has the same beginning sound. Encourage your child to say a sentence that uses both words. Finally invite your child to color the pictures.

Brock Goes Shopping

Directions: Invite your child to say nursery rhymes and identify the rhyming words. Then tell your child that Brock is going shopping to buy things that rhyme with his name. Ask your child to color the pictures whose names rhyme with *Brock*.

Rhyming Words
3-2-1 Learn, SV 9781419099281

Stack of Boxes

Directions: Stack three blocks or three boxes. Point out to your child the positions of top, middle, and bottom. Then have your child use a red crayon to color the top box, a blue crayon to color the middle box, and a yellow crayon to color the bottom box. Invite your child to color the rest of the picture.

Going on a Picnic

Directions: Line up three stuffed animals. Use them to point out to your child the positions of before, after, and between. Then have your child look at the top picture. Ask your child to use a pink crayon to color the animal that is *before* the turtle and a green crayon to color the animal that is *after* the pig. Finally have your child look at the bottom picture. Ask your child to use an orange crayon to color the animal that is *between* two animals.

Breakfast Time

Directions: Show your child three fruits or vegetables, two of which are about the same size. Ask your child to point to the ones that are the same size. Then have your child color the two foods that are the same size in each box. Next invite your child to color the picture.

Same Size
3-2-1 Learn, SV 9781419099281

Clothes Pairs

Directions: Show your child several pairs of socks and shoes. Point out that each pair is the same color. Then have your child color each pair of clothing the same color. Next invite your child to color the picture.

In the Kitchen

Directions: Show your child two forks and a spoon. Have your child point to the tools that are the same shape. Then invite your child to color the objects that are the same shape. Next invite your child to color the picture.

Same Shape
3-2-1 Learn, SV 9781419099281

Blast Off!

Directions: Show your child three leaves, two of which are the same kind. Have your child point to the leaf that is different. Then have your child use a pencil or crayon to write an **X** on each sun and moon that is different. Next invite your child to color the rest of the picture.

A Cherry Bird

Directions: Draw a circle and have your child trace it. Take your child on a hunt around the house to find more circles. Then have your child color the circles at the top of the page. Invite your child to use a pencil or crayon to trace the circles and color the picture.

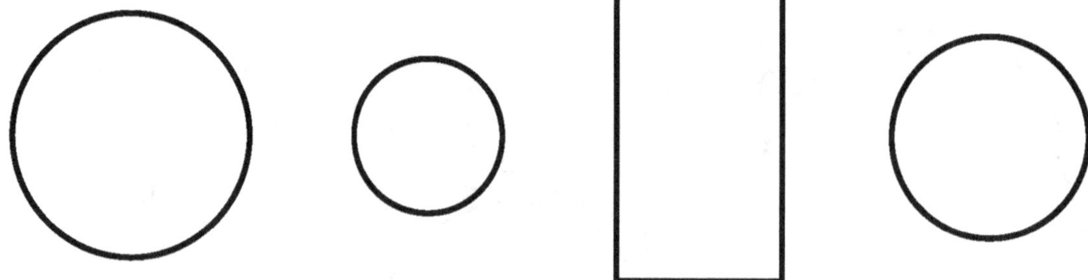

Circles
3-2-1 Learn, SV 9781419099281

Look in the Windows

Directions: Draw a rectangle and have your child trace it. Take your child on a hunt around the house to find more rectangles. Then have your child color the rectangles at the top of the page. Invite your child to use a pencil or crayon to trace the rectangles and color the picture.

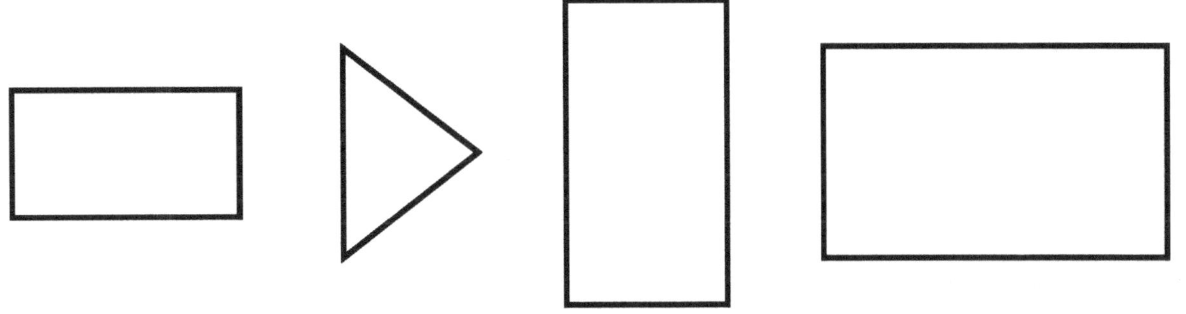

Rectangles
3-2-1 Learn, SV 9781419099281

Fish Tails

Directions: Draw a triangle and have your child trace it. Take your child on a hunt around the house to find more triangles. Then have your child color the triangles at the top of the page. Invite your child to use a pencil or crayon to trace the triangles and color the picture.

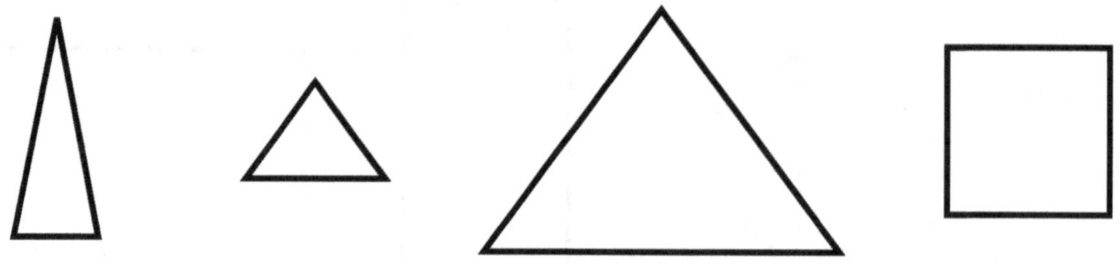

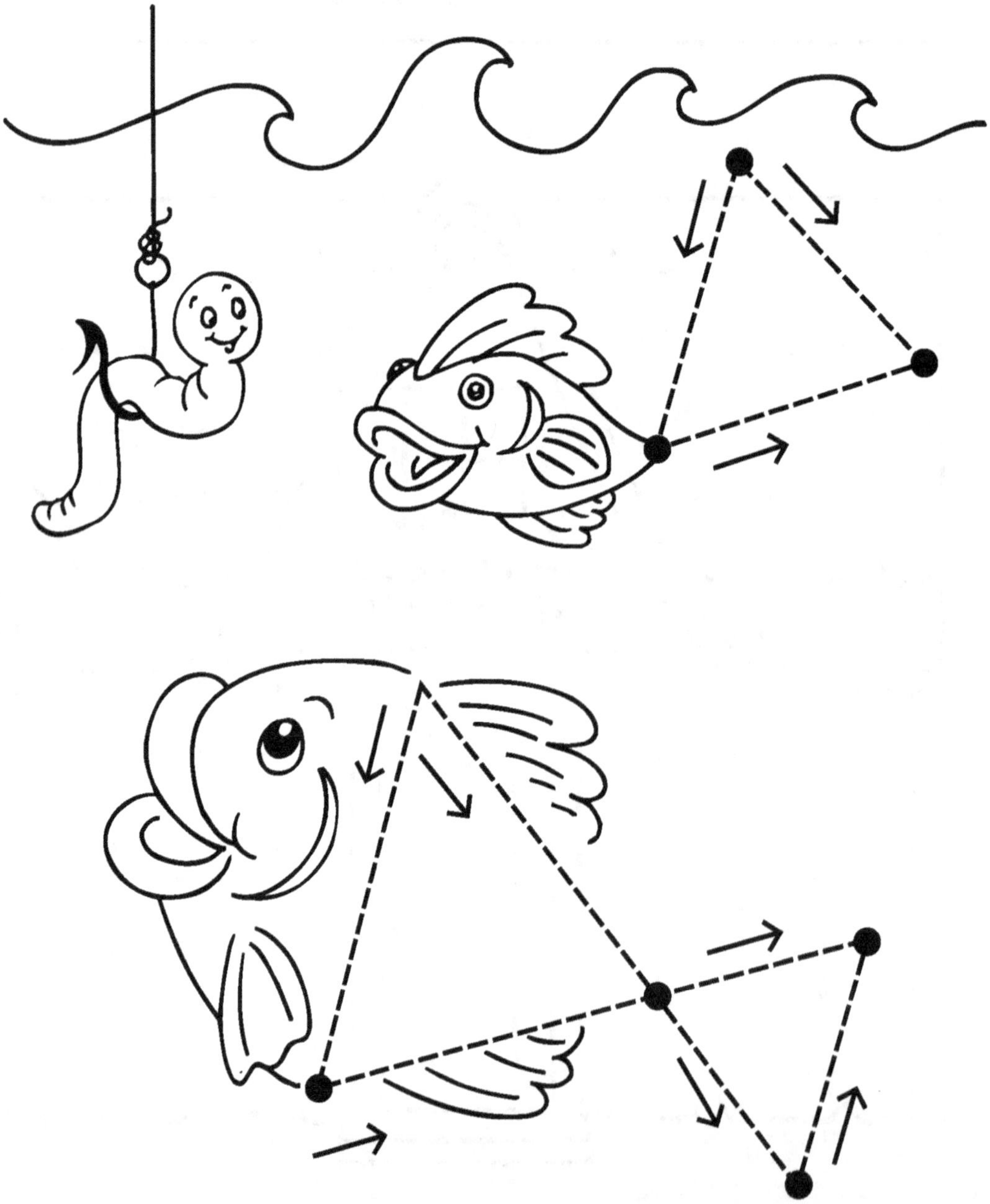

Triangles
3-2-1 Learn, SV 9781419099281

Build with Blocks

Directions: Draw a square and have your child trace it. Take your child on a hunt around the house to find more squares. Then have your child color the squares at the top of the page. Invite your child to use a pencil or crayon to trace the squares and color the picture.

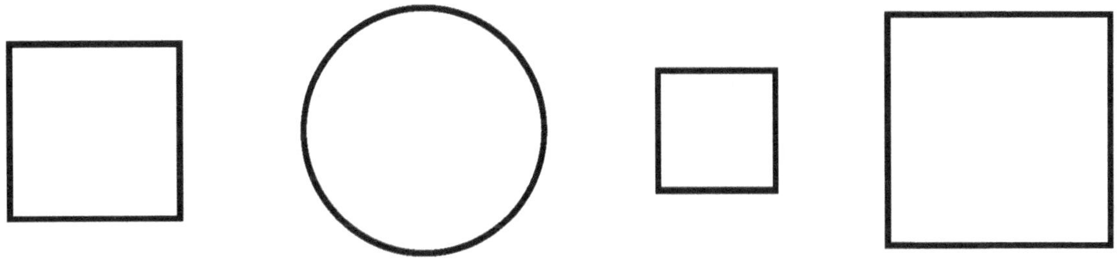

49

Squares
3-2-1 Learn, SV 9781419099281

One Horse

Directions: Give your child one object and say the number name. Then have your child count the horse and use a pencil or crayon to trace the number. Finally ask your child to color the pictures that show one haystack and write the number *1*.

one

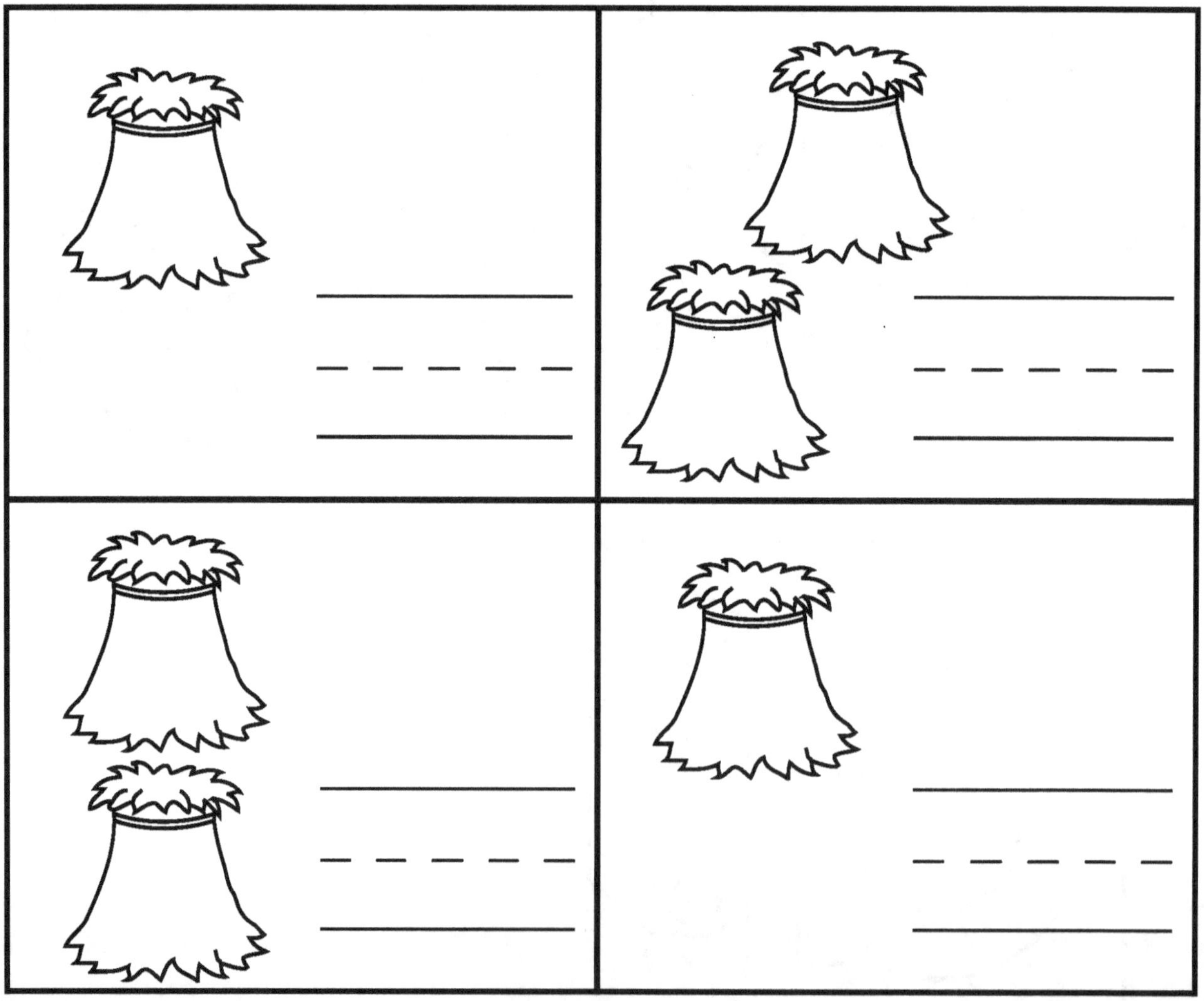

Two Bears

Directions: Give your child two objects and say the number name. Then have your child count the bears and use a pencil or crayon to trace the number. Finally ask your child to color the pictures that show two honey jars and write the number 2.

two

2 2

Number 2
3-2-1 Learn, SV 9781419099281

Three Cats

Directions: Give your child three objects and say the number name. Then have your child count the cats and use a pencil or crayon to trace the number. Finally ask your child to color the pictures that show three balls of yarn and write the number *3*.

three

3 3

Number 3
3-2-1 Learn, SV 9781419099281

Four Dogs

four

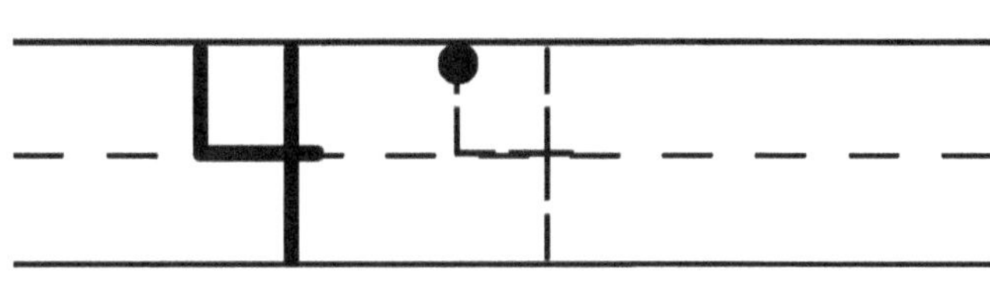

Five Rabbits

Directions: Give your child five objects and say the number name. Then have your child count the rabbits and use a pencil or crayon to trace the number. Finally ask your child to color the pictures that show five carrots and write the number *5*.

five

5 5

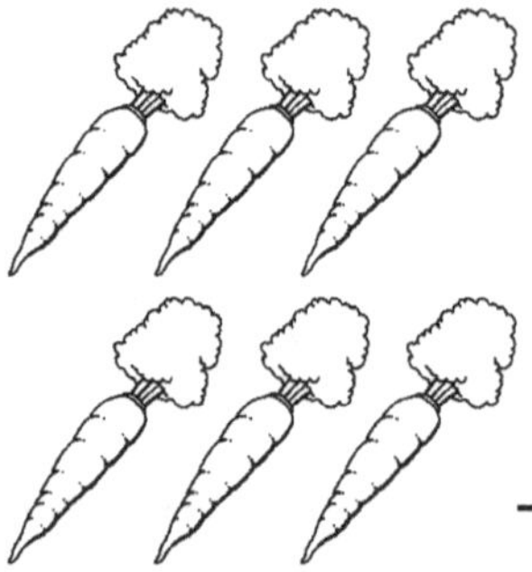

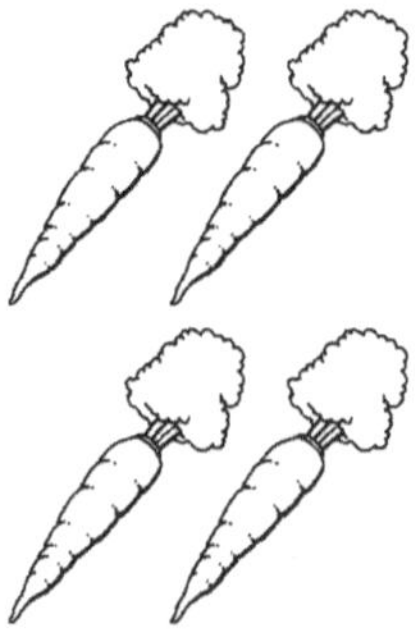

Number 5
3-2-1 Learn, SV 9781419099281

A Monkey Review

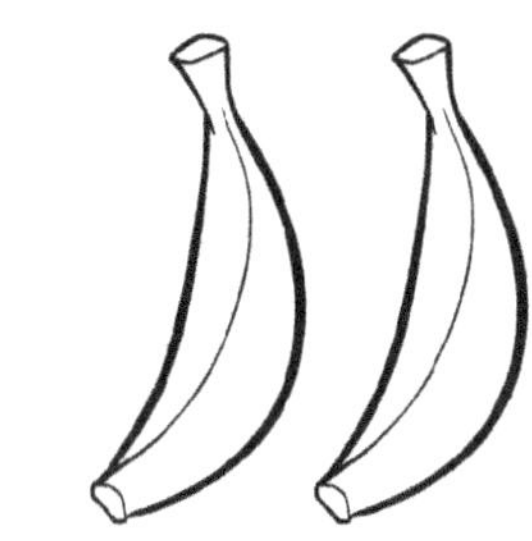

2 3

3 4

1 2

4 5

2 3

Six Fish

Directions: Give your child six objects and say the number name. Then have your child count the fish and use a pencil or crayon to trace the number. Finally ask your child to color the pictures that show six fishbowls and write the number *6*.

six

Number 6
3-2-1 Learn, SV 9781419099281

Seven Bees

Directions: Give your child seven objects and say the number name. Then have your child count the bees and use a pencil or crayon to trace the number. Finally ask your child to color the pictures that show seven hives and write the number 7.

seven

7 7

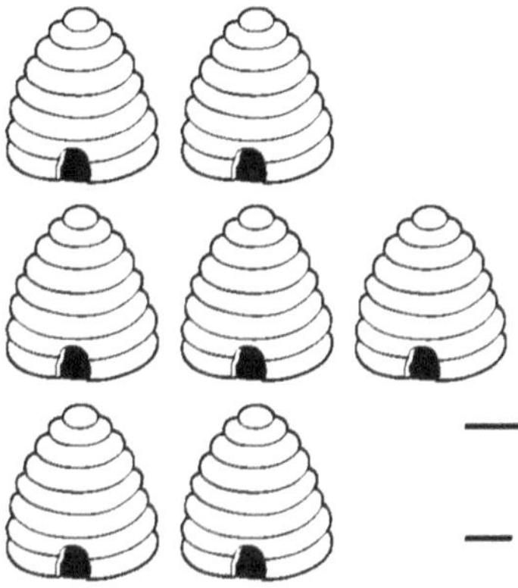

Number 7
3-2-1 Learn, SV 9781419099281

Eight Birds

Directions: Give your child eight objects and say the number name. Then have your child count the birds and use a pencil or crayon to trace the number. Finally ask your child to color the pictures that show eight nests and write the number 8.

eight

8   8

3-2-1 Learn, SV 9781419099281

Nine Butterflies

Directions: Give your child nine objects and say the number name. Then have your child count the butterflies and use a pencil or crayon to trace the number. Finally ask your child to color the pictures that show nine flowers and write the number 9.

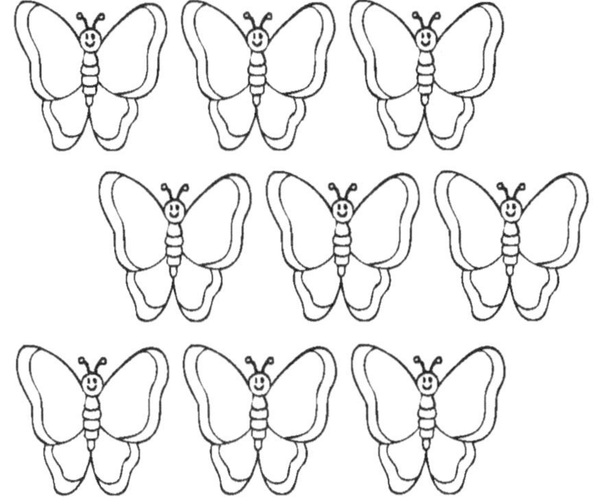

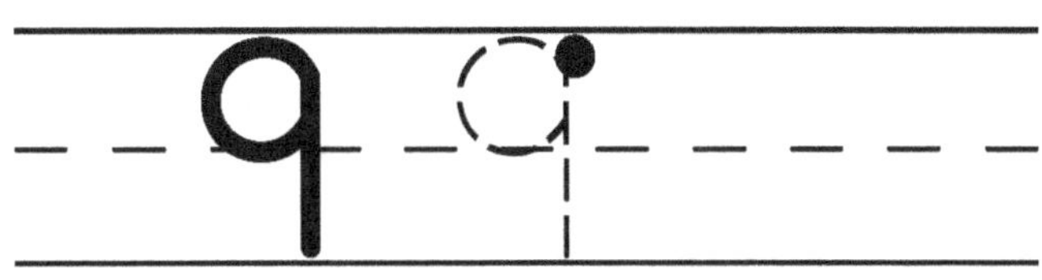

nine

9

Ten Ladybugs

Directions: Give your child ten objects and say the number name. Then have your child count the ladybugs and use a pencil or crayon to trace the number. Finally ask your child to color the pictures that show ten leaves and write the number _10_.

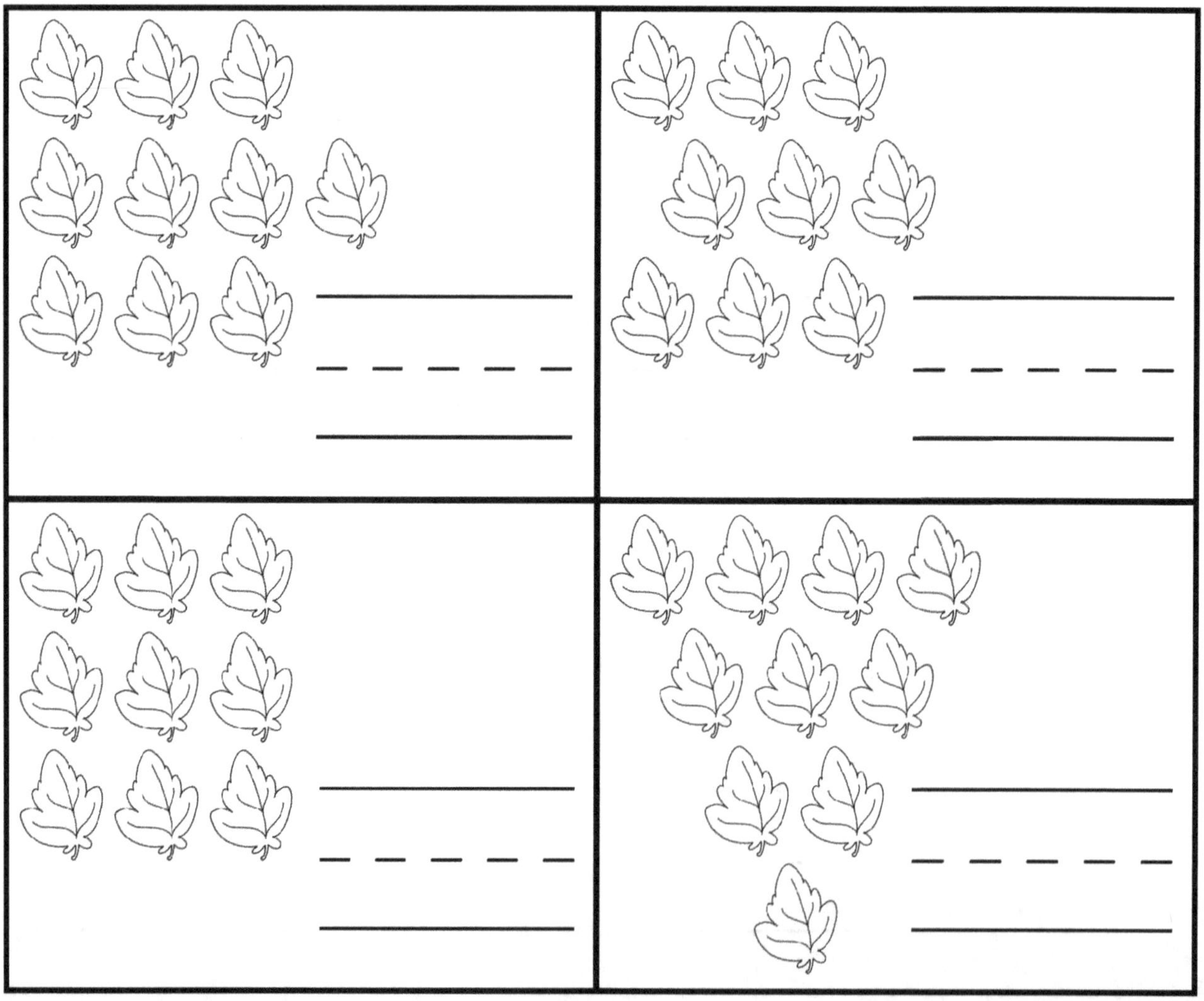

ten

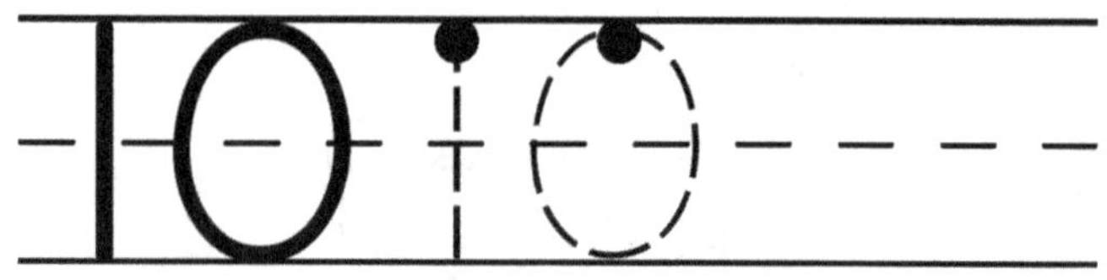

3-2-1 Learn, SV 9781419099281

A Nutty Review

Directions: Show your child a group of seven objects and ask him or her to tell how many. Then have your child use a pencil or crayon to circle the number to show how many nuts and write the number.

8 9

6 7

9 10

7 8

8 9

Review Numbers 6–10
3-2-1 Learn, SV 9781419099281

Vegetable Count

Directions: Help your child count ten pieces of cereal or small treats. Say the names of the numbers in order and ask your child to show that many. Then have your child color the vegetables to show the numbers.

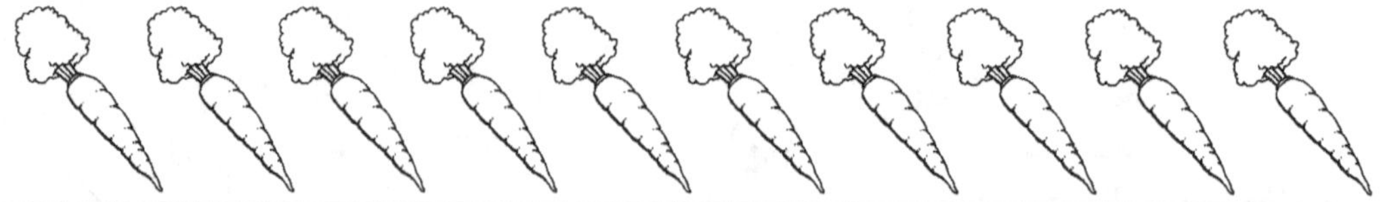

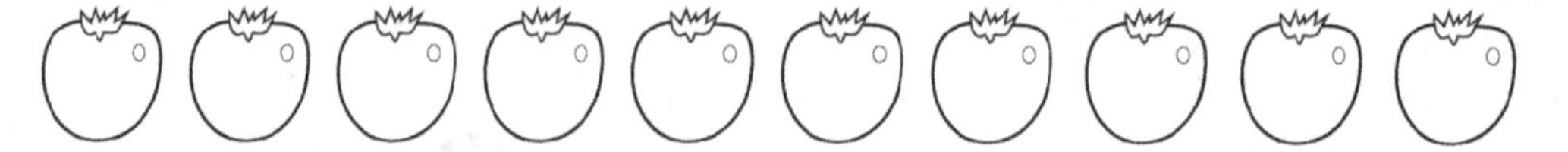

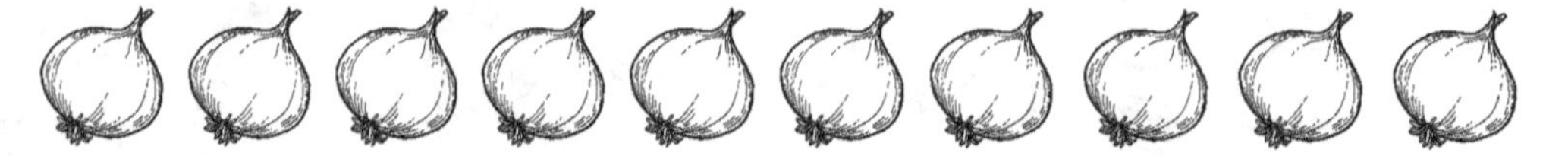

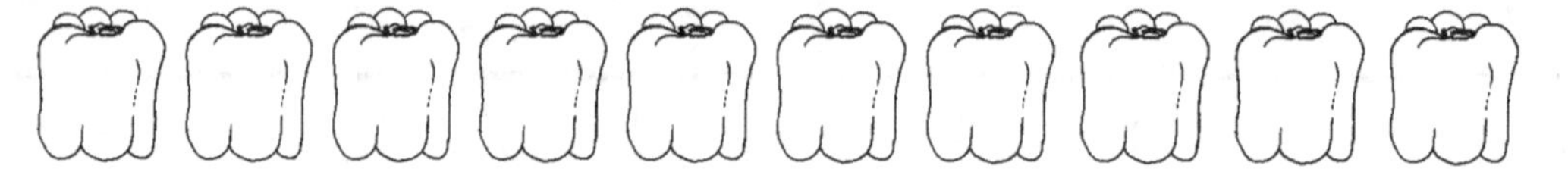

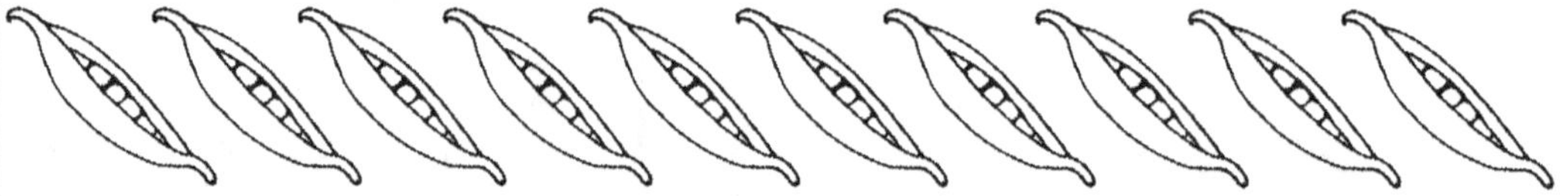

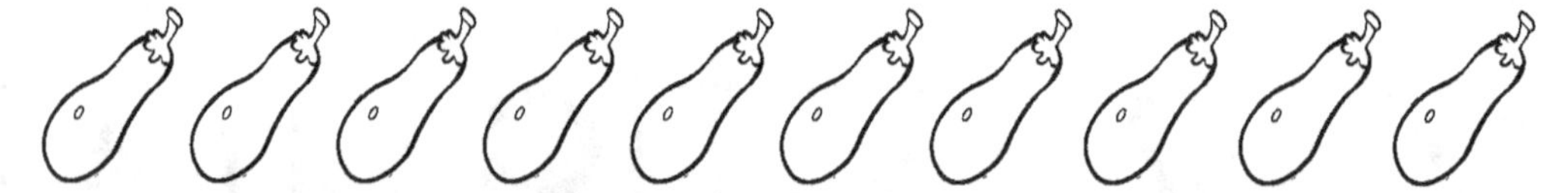

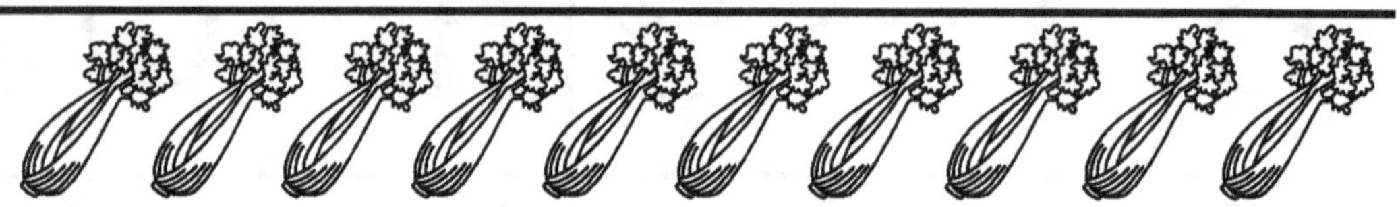

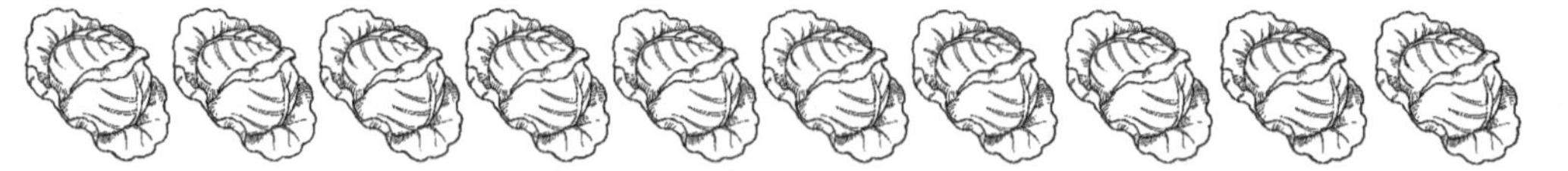

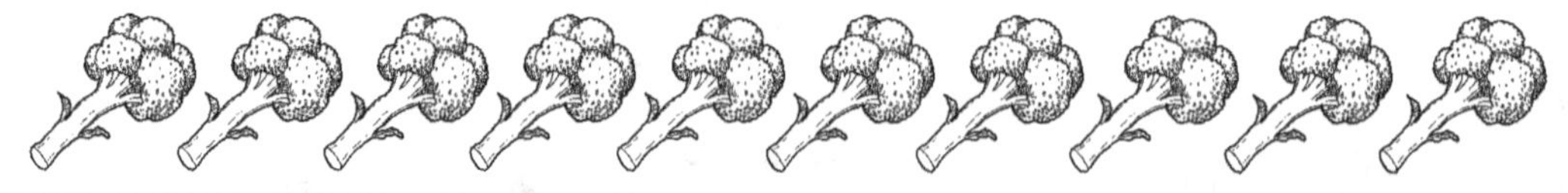

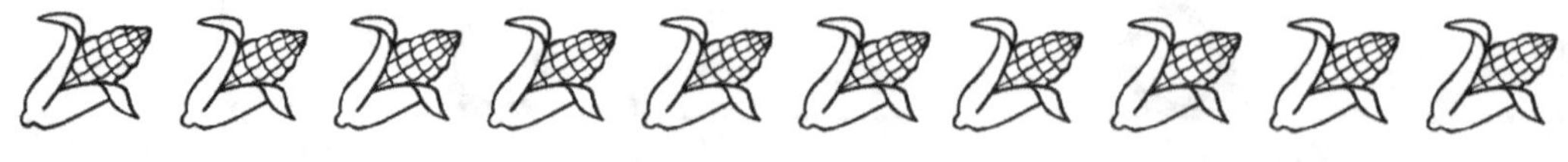

Going for a Ride

Directions: Show your child one to five objects. Ask your child to count them and show another group of objects that is the same. Then have your child count the animals or objects in each group. Tell your child to use a pencil or crayon to draw a line between equal groups. Finally invite your child to color the page.

Equal Groups
3-2-1 Learn, SV 9781419099281

Fewer Toys

Directions: Show your child one to ten toys. Ask your child to count them and show another group of toys that has fewer. Then have your child count each group of toys. Tell your child to use a pencil or crayon to draw a group that has fewer. Finally invite your child to color the page.

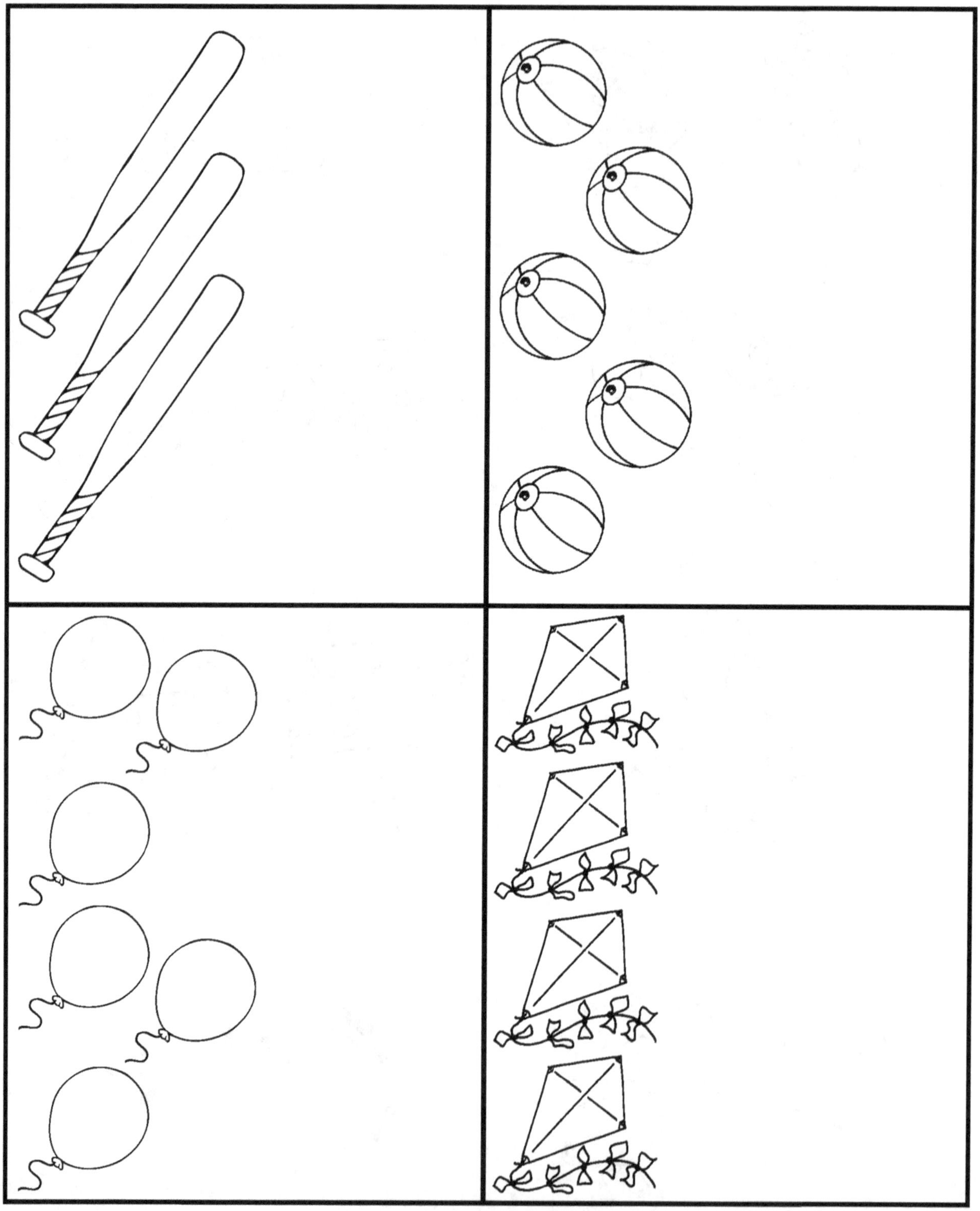

Fewer
3-2-1 Learn, SV 9781419099281

More Shapes

Directions: Cut out ten circles. Show your child a group of four circles. Ask your child to count them and show another group of circles that has more. Then have your child count each group of shapes. Tell your child to use a pencil or crayon to draw a group that has more. Finally invite your child to color the page.

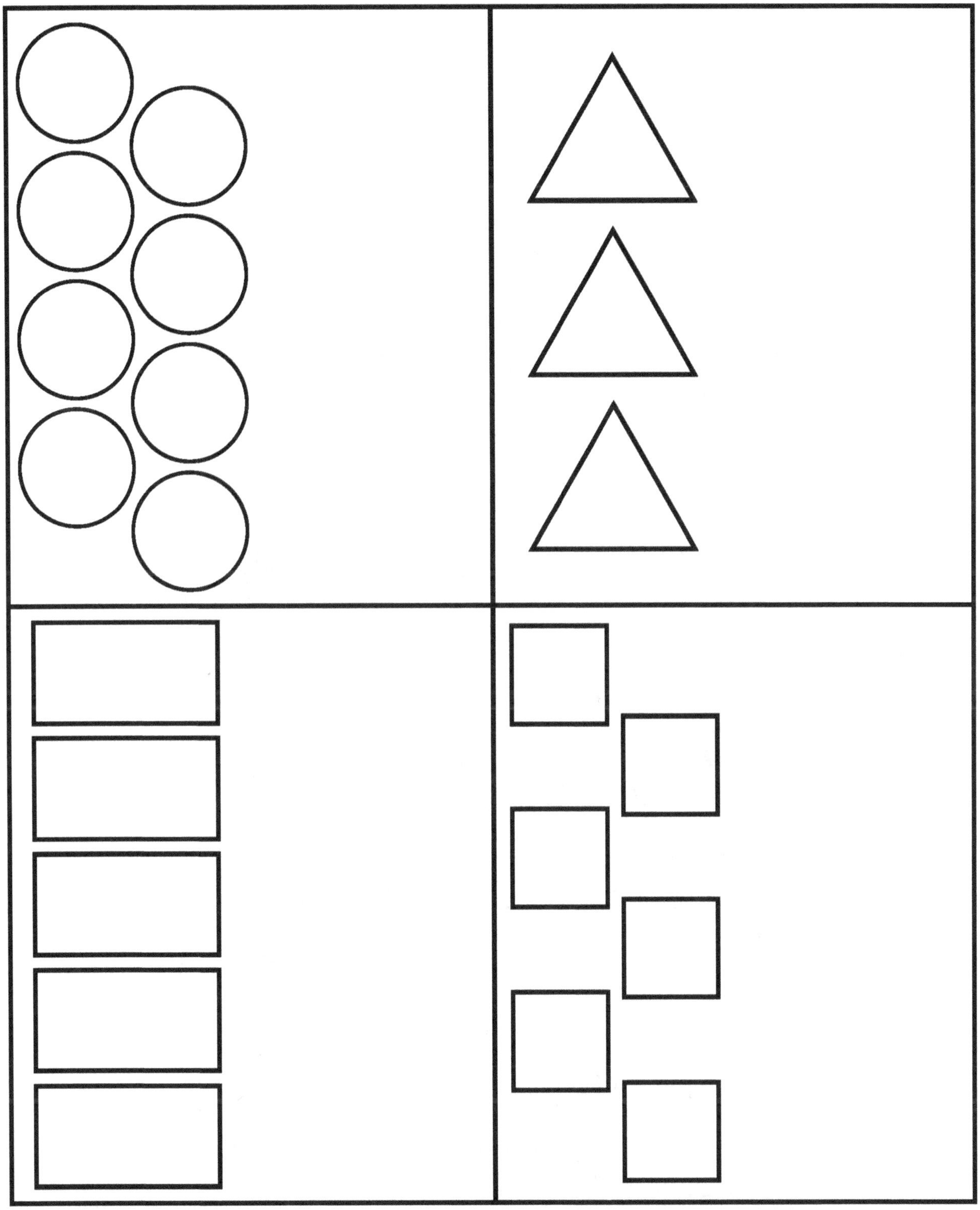

More
3-2-1 Learn, SV 9781419099281

Hungry Ant

Directions: Write the numbers *1* to *10* on separate cards. Invite your child to put them in order. Then ask your child to lead the ant to the apple by drawing a line to show the numbers in order.

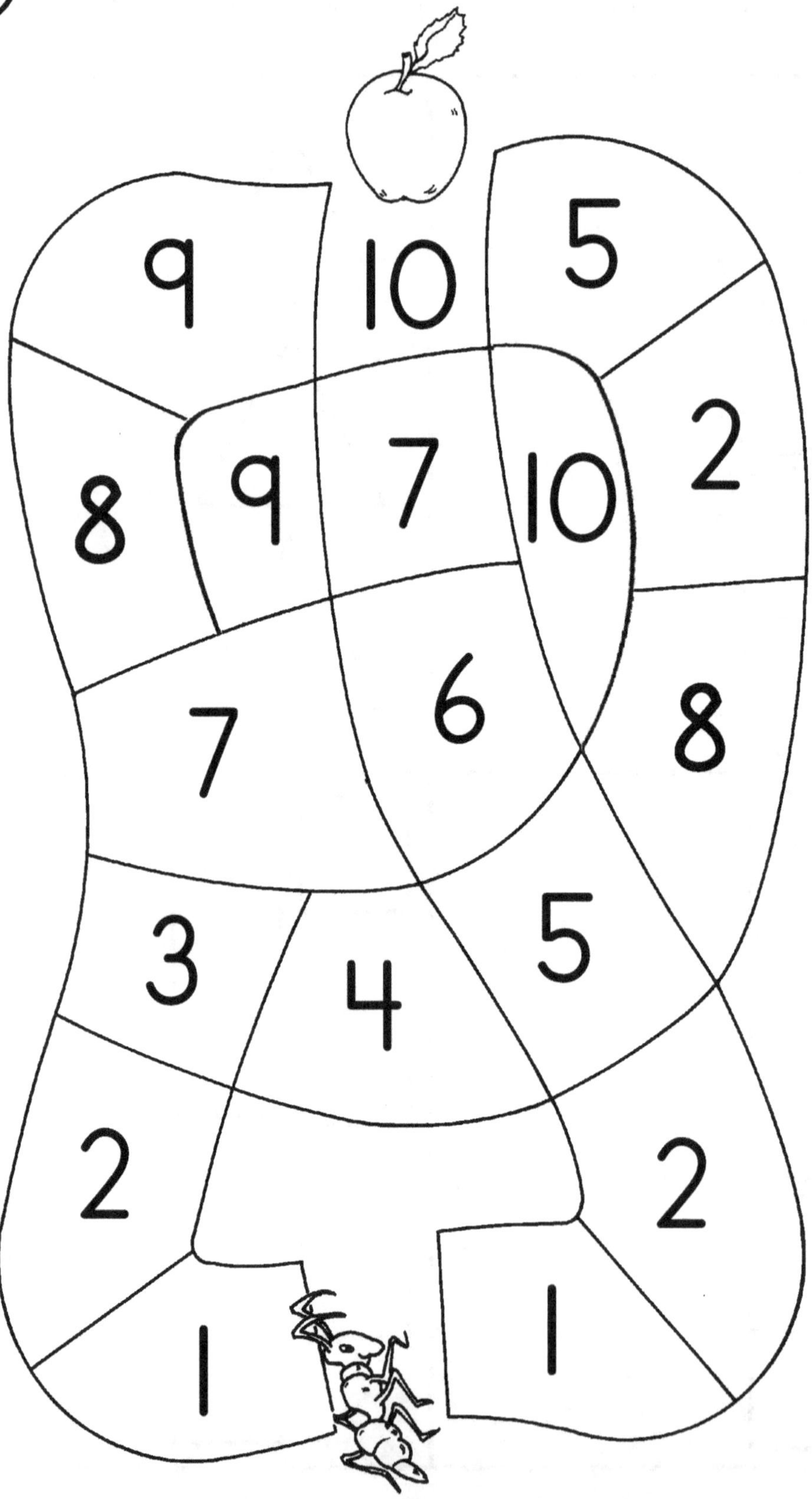

Order Numbers to 10
3-2-1 Learn, SV 9781419099281

Arts and Crafts

Directions: Show your child two pencils that are different lengths. Ask your child to tell which one is longer and which one is shorter. Then have your child use a blue crayon to color the longer object in each pair and a yellow crayon to color the shorter one.

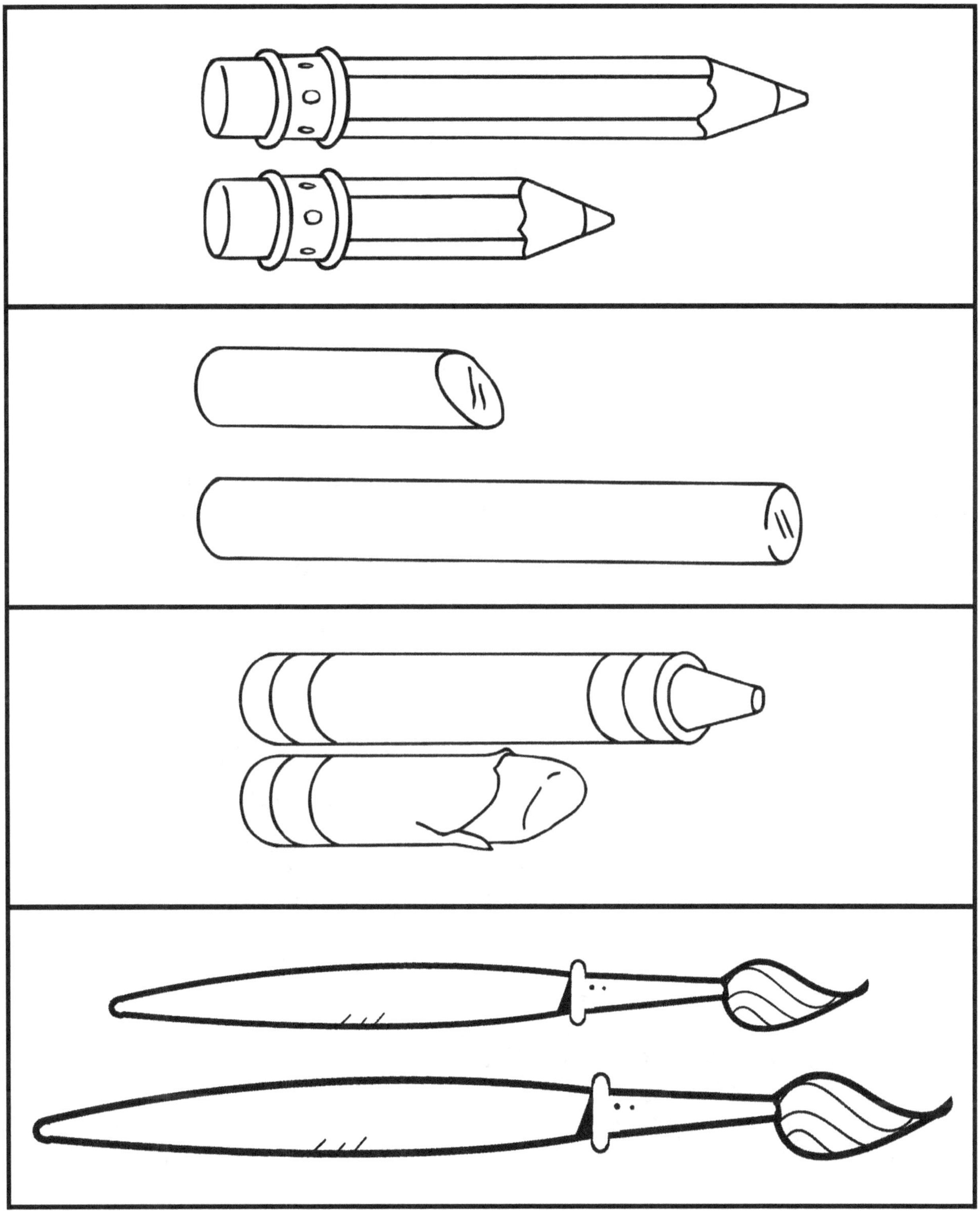

Long and Short
3-2-1 Learn, SV 9781419099281

Clowning Around

Directions: Show your child two balls that are different sizes. Have your child tell which one is big and which one is little. Then ask your child to use a blue crayon to circle the little clown, little balloon, and little ball and use a red crayon to circle the big clown, big balloon, and big ball. Invite your child to color the picture.

Big and Little
3-2-1 Learn, SV 9781419099281

Hot or Cold

Directions: Fill a mug with warm water and another with ice water. Have your child tell which one is hot and which one is cold. Then ask your child to use a red crayon to circle the objects that are hot and a blue crayon to circle the ones that are cold. Invite your child to color the pictures.

Hold It

Hop Home, Rabbit

Directions: Take a walk with your child to collect four leaves from two different trees. Arrange them in a variety of patterns and have your child name the pattern. Then ask your child to lead the rabbit to its home following a leaf pattern. Have your child use an orange crayon and a red crayon to show the leaf pattern the rabbit follows.

Patterns
3-2-1 Learn, SV 9781419099281

Animals on Parade

Directions: Arrange six stuffed animals or dolls in a row. Point out to your child their order from first to sixth. Then have your child use a pencil or crayon to draw a line above the animal that is first, circle the animal that is third, and draw an **X** on the animal that is fourth. Invite your child to color the picture.

3-2-1 Learn, SV 9781419099281

We Belong Together

Classify
3-2-1 Learn, SV 9781419099281

Is It Living?

Directions: Take a walk with your child and find things that are living and nonliving. Point out that living things breathe, need food, and grow. Then have your child use a pencil or crayon to circle the living things and color the pictures.

Living and Nonliving Things
3-2-1 Learn, SV 9781419099281

We Need

Directions: Tell your child that all living things need air to breathe, food to eat, and water to drink. Then have your child use a pencil or crayon to trace the objects and color the pictures.

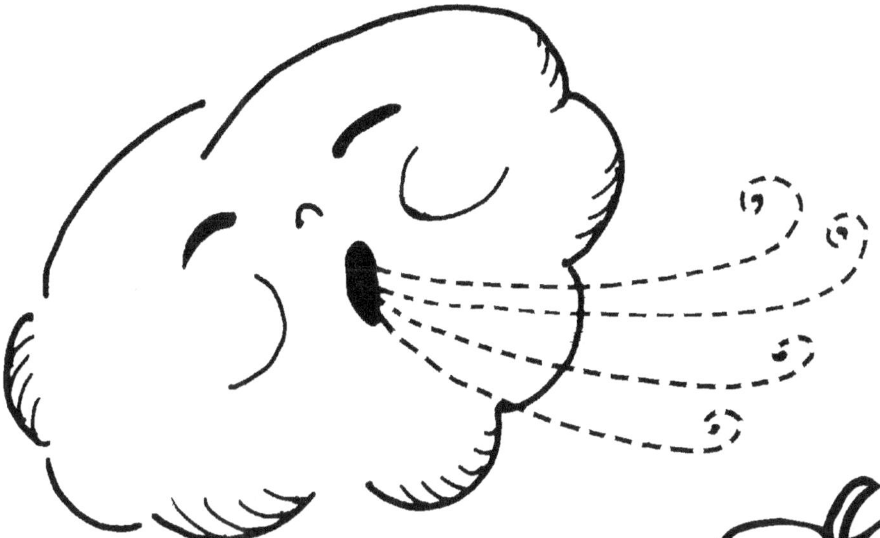

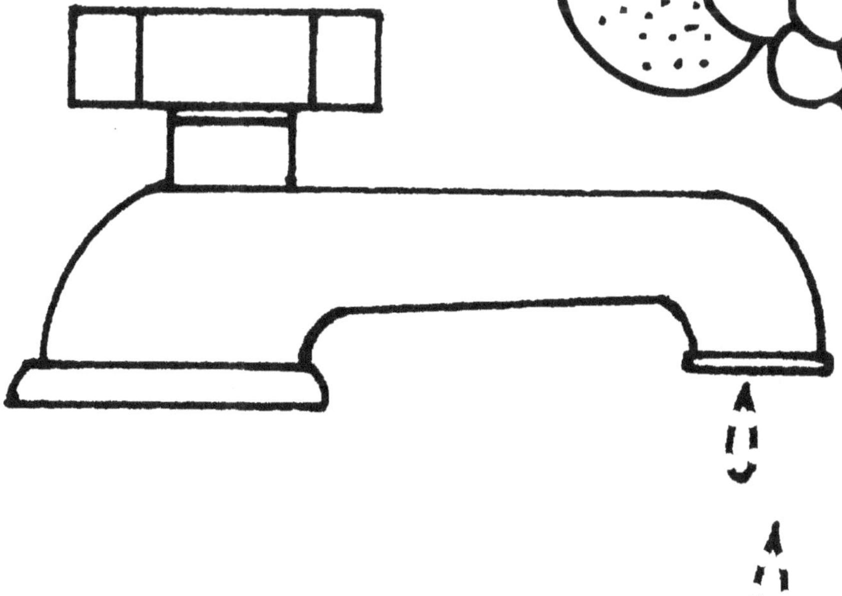

Needs of Living Things
3-2-1 Learn, SV 9781419099281

Growing Up

Directions: Show your child a picture of a puppy or kitten. Discuss how the puppy changes as it gets older. Then tell your child that all living things grow and change. Have your child use a pencil or crayon to draw a line from each young animal or plant to what it looks like in the middle of its life cycle and what it looks like at the end of its life cycle. The first one is done for you.

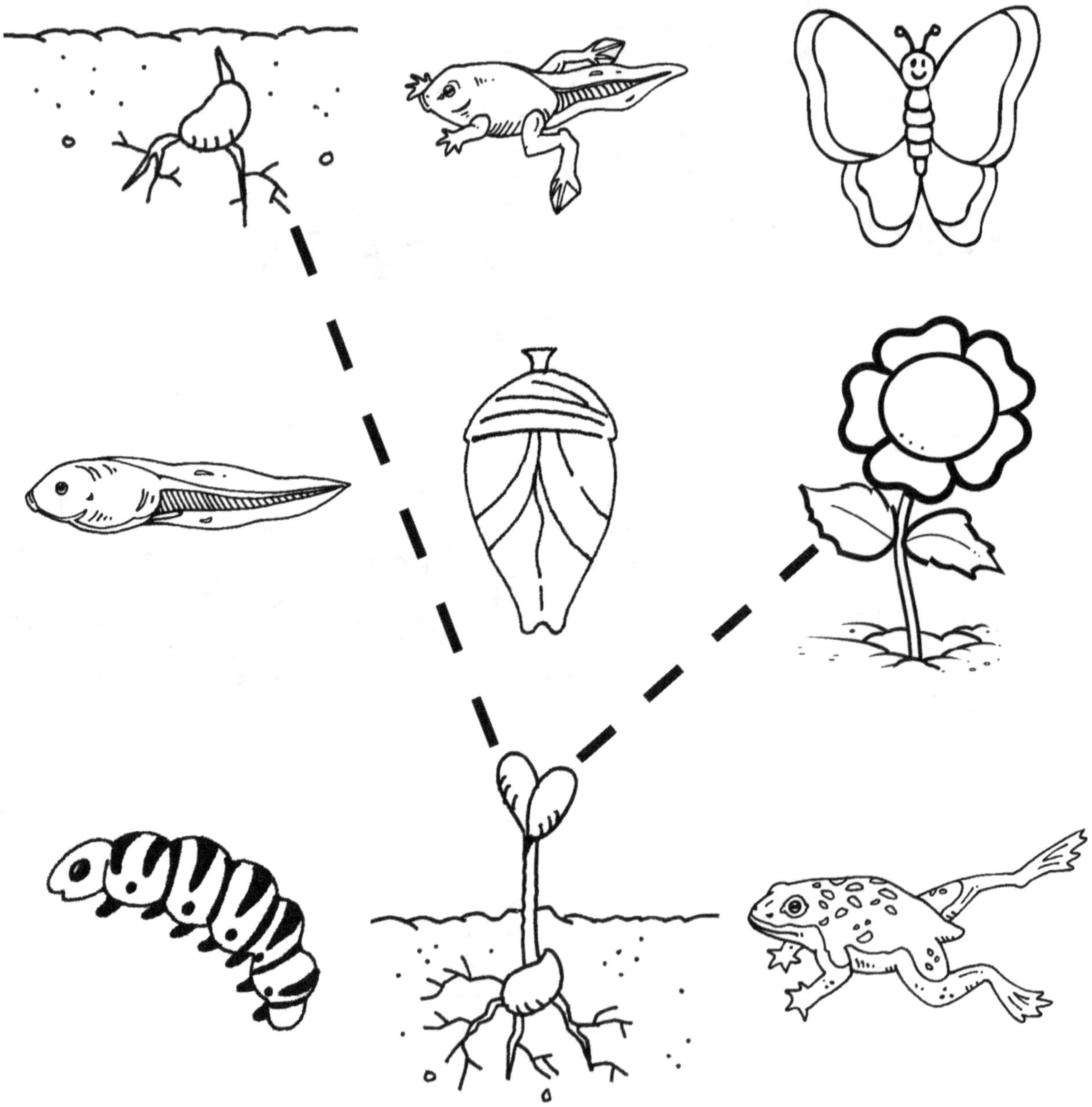

Animals All Around

Home, Sweet Home

Directions: Take a walk with your child to look for places animals live. Discuss how the home is a safe place for them to live. Then ask your child to name the animals that live in the places you see on your walk. Have your child look closely at the forest scene to see where each animal might live. Invite your child to use a pencil or crayon to draw a line from each animal to that place. Finally invite your child to color the pictures.

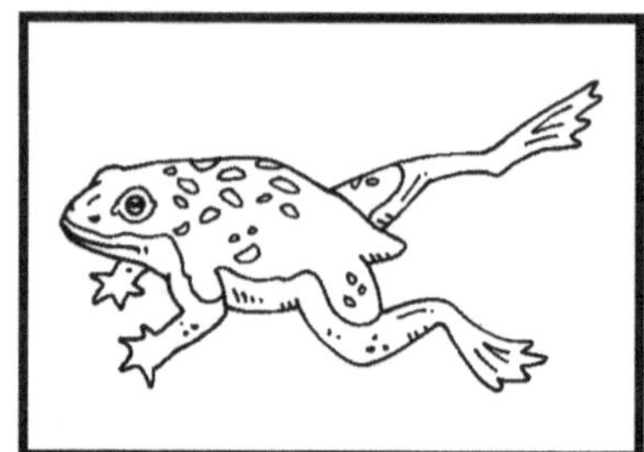

Where Animals Live
3-2-1 Learn, SV 9781419099281

Useful Parts

Directions: Invite your child to look at your pet or a neighbor's pet. Discuss the different parts and how they help the animal. Then have your child look at each animal, use a pencil or crayon to draw the missing part, and color it. Discuss how the part helps the animal.

Parts That Help Animals
3-2-1 Learn, SV 9781419099281

Safety First!

Directions: Ask your child to watch a bird. Discuss how it flies up into a tree to stay safe. Then have your child look at each animal and use a pencil or crayon to circle the part that helps it stay safe. Discuss why. Finally invite your child to color the pictures.

80

Parts That Help Animals Stay Safe
3-2-1 Learn, SV 9781419099281

Get Going

Directions: Name animals and invite your child to move like that animal. Then ask your child to use a pencil or crayon to draw lines to connect two animals that move in the same way. Invite your child to color the pictures.

Plants All Around

Directions: Invite your child to take a walk to look at plants and their parts. Discuss how the plants you see on your walk are alike and different. Then have your child color the plants in the picture.

Fine Flowers

Directions: Point out the roots, stem, leaves, and flowers of a plant and discuss their functions with your child. Then have your child use a pencil or crayon to draw the part that is missing on each flower. Invite your child to color the picture.

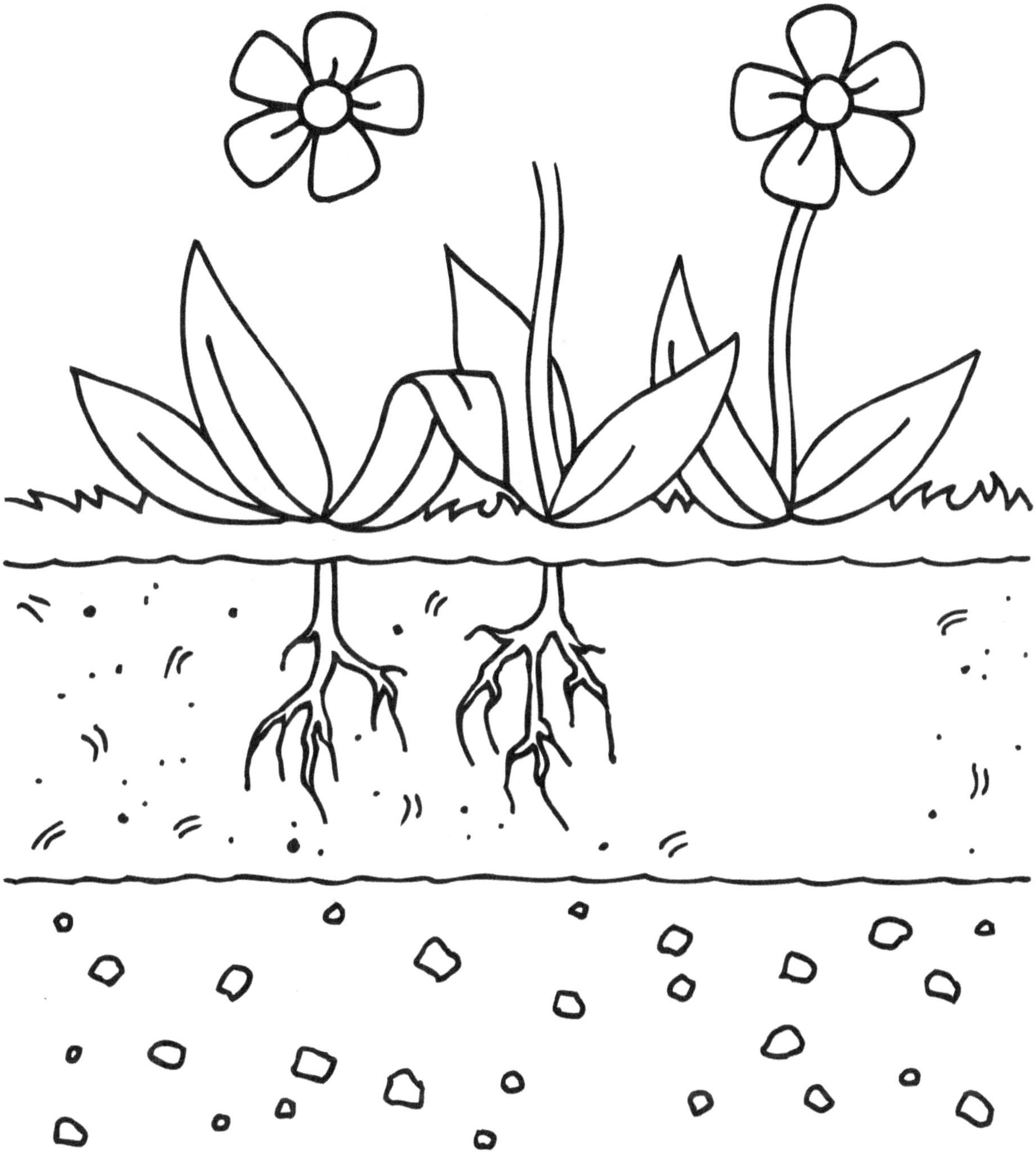

Seed Count

Directions: Invite your child to have a fruit snack. Cut open the fruit for your child and point out the seeds. Explain that seeds can be planted to make new plants. Then have your child identify each food, count the seeds, and use a pencil or crayon to write the number of seeds there are in the food. Ask your child to color the pictures.

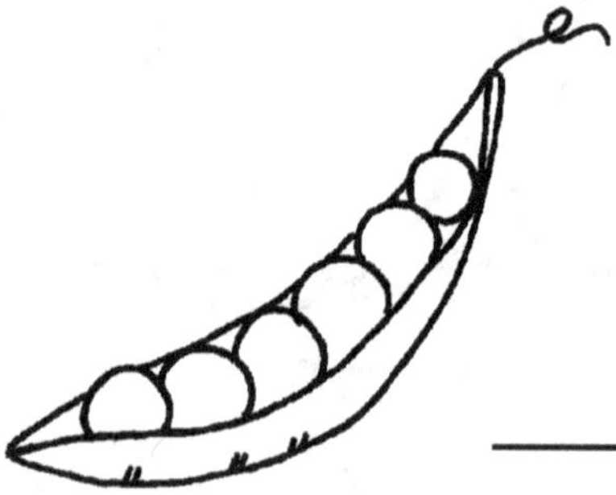

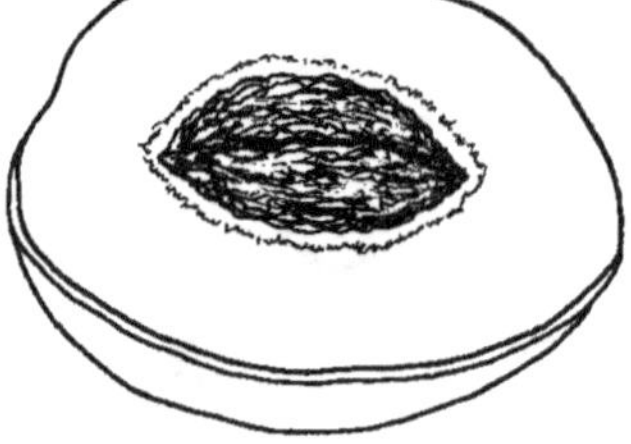

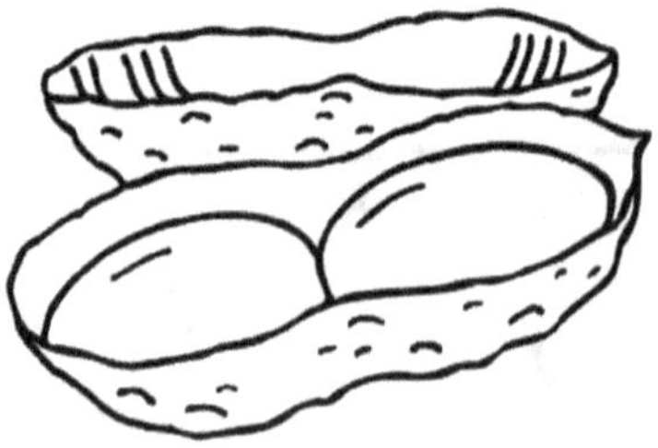

Seeds
3-2-1 Learn, SV 9781419099281

Gifts from Nature

Directions: Show your child a cotton T-shirt. Explain that the material was made from a cotton plant. Then tell your child that people make and use many things from nature. Look around the house for other examples. Next invite your child to use a pencil or crayon to draw a line from each object to where it came from.

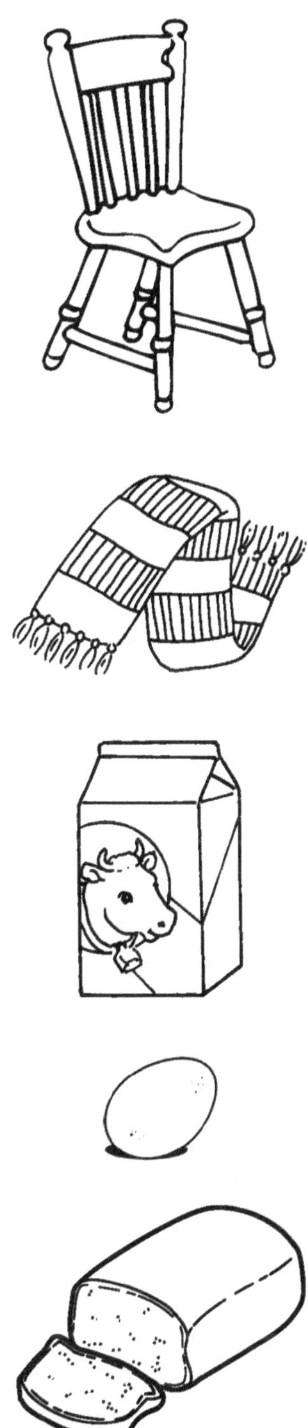

Parts of Me

Directions: Name the different body parts, such as eyes, head, hands, legs, feet, nose, and ears. Have your child point to each body part and tell what it does. Then have your child identify each missing body part and use a pencil or crayon to draw it. Invite your child to color the picture.

My Senses

Directions: Discuss the five senses with your child. As you name each sense, ask your child to tell what he or she likes to use that sense for. Then have your child look at each object and use a pencil or crayon to circle the senses they use to observe and describe each object. Invite your child to color the pictures.

Senses
3-2-1 Learn, SV 9781419099281

We Grow and Change

Directions: Show your child photos of yourself at different ages. Then tell your child that people grow and change. Have your child use a pencil or crayon to write the numbers *1* to *4* to show the correct order of human growth.

Humans Grow and Change
3-2-1 Learn, SV 9781419099281

Good Food Maze

Directions: Invite your child to help pack a lunchbox for a picnic. Discuss the healthy foods that should be included. Explain that good foods help the body move. Then invite your child to help the girl pack her lunch by coloring the healthy foods along the path to the lunchbox.

Make Your Move

Directions: Lead your child in a set of exercises. Discuss how exercise helps make the muscles strong. Then invite your child to color the pictures that show children exercising.

Exercise
3-2-1 Learn, SV 9781419099281

Here's to Your Health

Directions: Read a book about tooth care to your child. Then invite your child to brush his or her teeth. Discuss other healthy practices your child follows. Have your child use a pencil or crayon to color the picture in each row that shows a healthy practice.

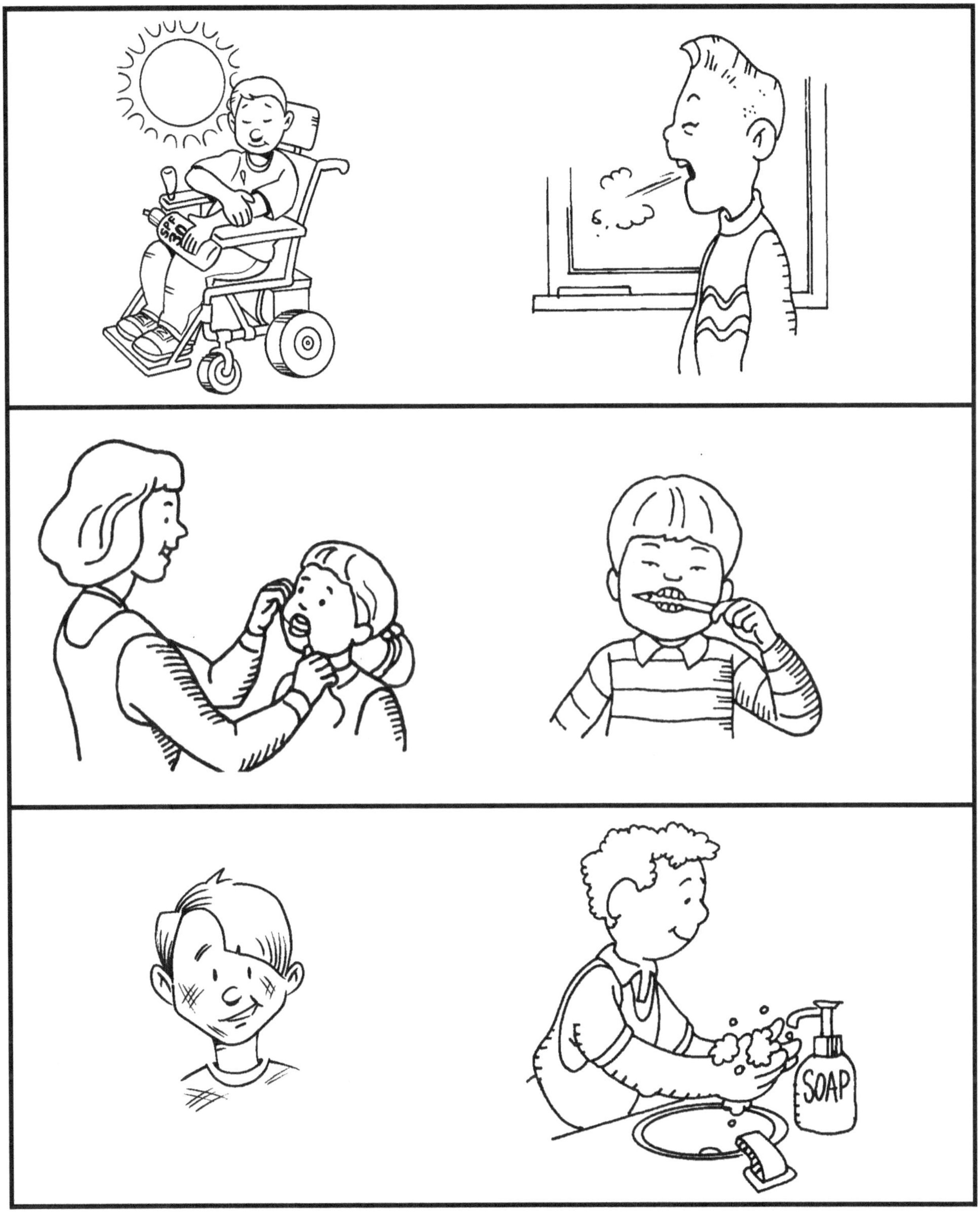

Call for Help

Directions: Talk with your child about the different kinds of emergencies that require adult help. Then show your child how to dial 911 on an unplugged phone. Practice the information your child should share, such as name, address, and telephone number. Next invite your child to use a pencil or crayon to draw a line connecting the numbers *1* to *10* in the correct order to make the receiver. Ask your child to trace the large emergency numbers and color the telephone.

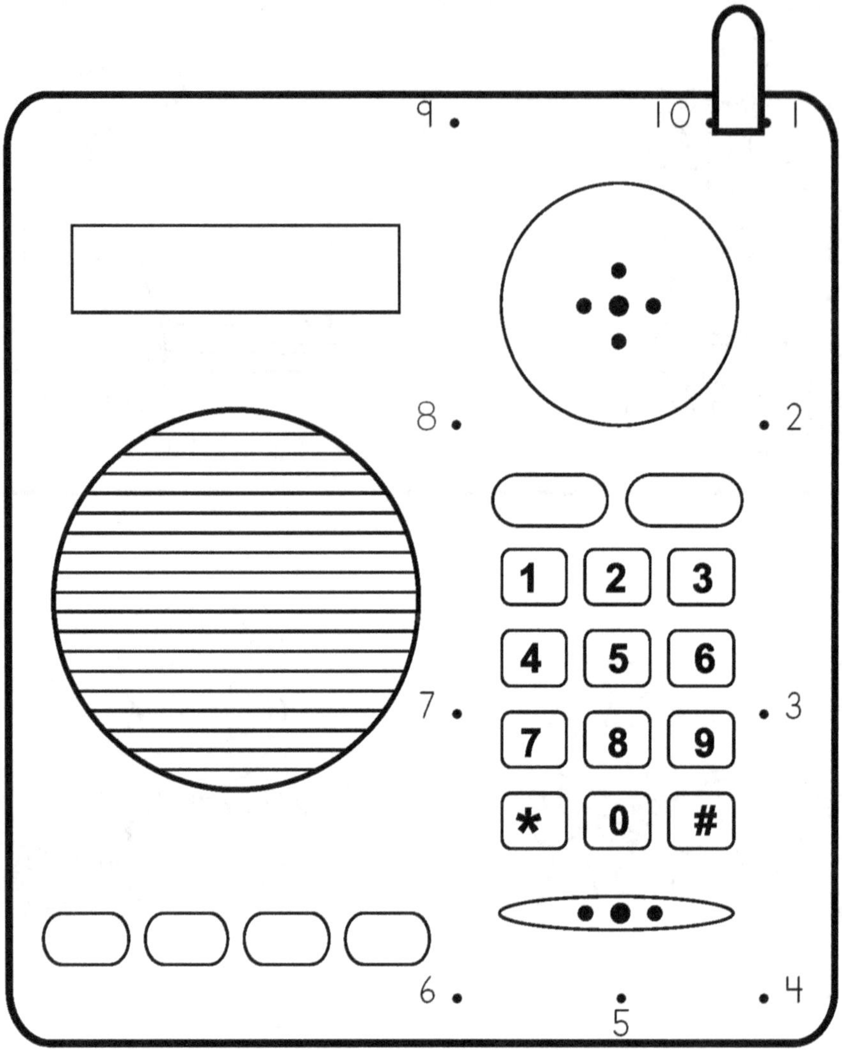

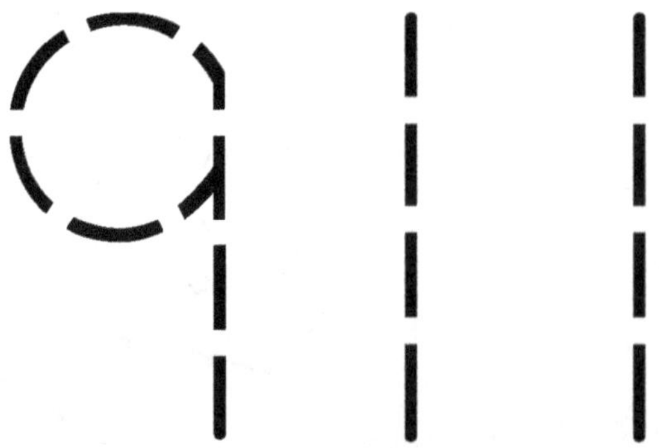

People Make Things

Directions: Show your child pictures of a bird nest and a house. Ask your child which one is made by nature and which one is made by people. Invite your child to go on a hunt in the neighborhood to find other things that are made by nature or made by people. Then have your child color the picture in each row that shows something made by people.

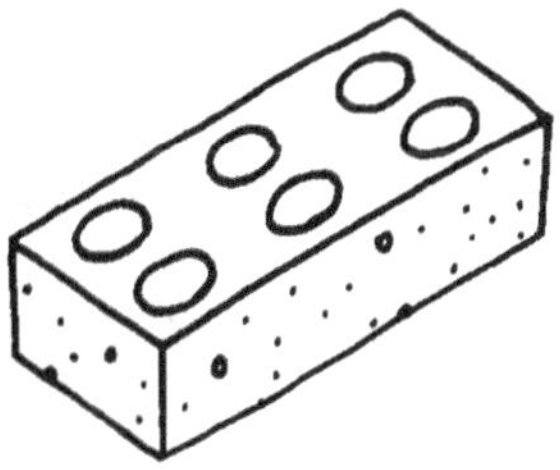

Natural or Man-made
3-2-1 Learn, SV 9781419099281

How Does It Feel?

Directions: Give your child a piece of cotton and ask him or her to find something else that feels soft like the cotton. As your child looks, point out other textures that are hard, rough, or smooth. Then ask your child to identify and color the first picture in each row. Have your child use a pencil or crayon to color another picture in the row that feels the same.

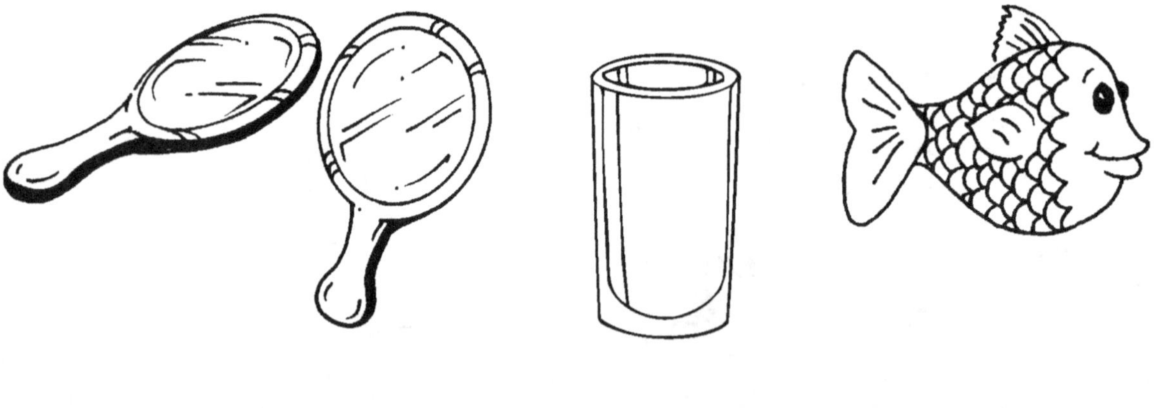

Classify Materials
3-2-1 Learn, SV 9781419099281

Weather Wear

Directions: Have your child look out a window and describe the weather. Ask your child what he or she will wear. Then have your child use a pencil or crayon to write an **X** on the person that is not dressed for the weather. Ask your child to color the picture.

Weather
3-2-1 Learn, SV 9781419099281

Seasons of Fun

Directions: Take a walk with your child and look for signs of the season. Point out activities that people are doing that pertain to the time of year. Then have your child identify the seasons by looking at the trees. Ask your child to use a pencil or crayon to draw lines to match the tree to the activity that can be done during that season.

Night and Day

Directions: Invite your child to look at the night sky and identify objects that can be seen only at night. Discuss what object can be seen in the day sky and how night and day differ. Then invite your child to use a pencil or crayon to draw objects in the window to show the correct time of day.

Night and Day
3-2-1 Learn, SV 9781419099281

Land and Water

Directions: With your child, page through picture books to find examples of Earth's landforms and water features, including mountains, rivers, and lakes. Discuss how they are alike and different. Then have your child use a brown crayon to color the mountains, a green crayon to color the hills, and a blue crayon to color the river and lake. Finally invite your child to color the rest of the picture.

Earth's Surface
3-2-1 Learn, SV 9781419099281

We Need Water

Resources Are Useful
3-2-1 Learn, SV 9781419099281

I Can Help

Directions: Explain to your child that some things in our world are being used up very quickly, such as gas for cars, water for growing plants, and trees for building houses. Talk about ways that your family helps keep these things safe by recycling, reusing, or reducing. Then have your child color the picture in each row that shows how a child is helping.

Conserve Resources
3-2-1 Learn, SV 9781419099281

It's Stuck

Directions: Show your child a magnet and discuss that it has a special force that makes it stick to objects made of metal. Allow time for your child to experiment with objects that the magnet sticks to. Then show your child the objects on the page. Ask your child to guess which ones the magnet will stick to and place a dot by them. Have your child find the objects in your house and experiment by placing the magnet next to each one. Ask him or her to color the pictures of the objects that are attracted to the magnet. Discuss the results of the experiment and invite your child to color the picture of the children.

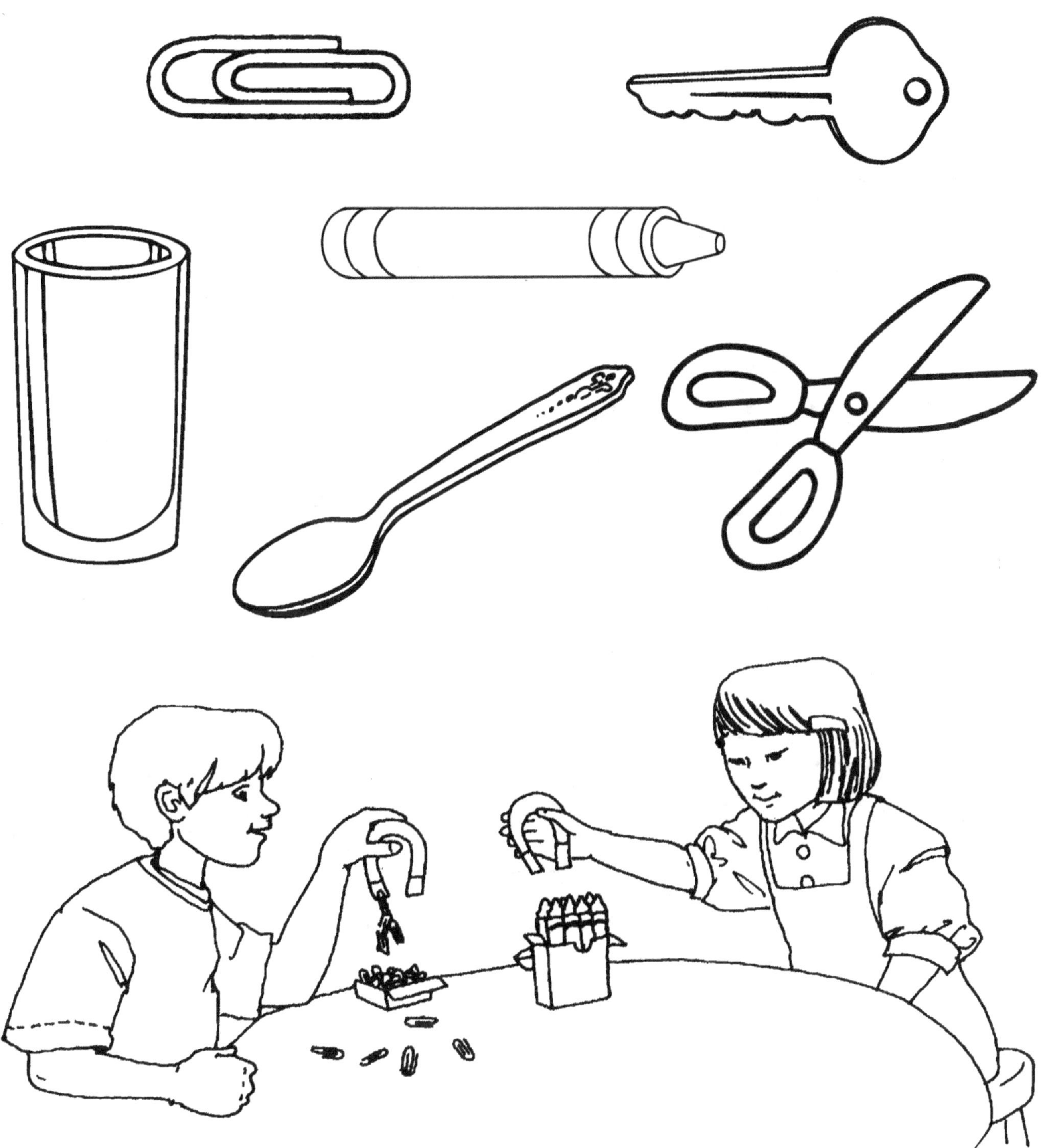

Characteristics of Magnets
3-2-1 Learn, SV 9781419099281

Air Is Everywhere

Directions: Ask your child to take a big breath and hold it for a few seconds. Explain that your child took air into his or her body. Then tell your child that a balloon can hold air, too. Explain that air can take the shape of anything it fills. Have your child look at the picture and use a pencil or crayon to circle all the things that have air inside them. Invite your child to color the picture.

Characteristics of Air
3-2-1 Learn, SV 9781419099281

Going Down

Directions: Visit a playground and ask your child to slide down the slide. Discuss how your child's body moves to the ground. As your child plays, point out other times that his or her body moves to the ground. Explain that gravity, a pull, makes all things move down to the ground. Then have your child look at each picture and use a pencil or crayon to draw an arrow to show how each object will move.

Gravity

3-2-1 Learn, SV 9781419099281

Clowning Around

Directions: Have your child spread out both hands and place them on the top half of the page. Use a pencil to trace the hands. Point out how the pointer finger and thumb form a capital "L" on the left hand. Have your child trace the fingers to make the *L*. Explain that the word *left* begins with L. Develop an understanding of left and right by asking your child to move either the left or right hand, arm, leg, or foot. Then tell your child to use a pencil or crayon to draw a balloon in the clown's right hand and an umbrella in the left hand.

Left and Right
3-2-1 Learn, SV 9781419099281

Horse Play

Directions: While taking a walk with your child, discuss the concepts of near and far. Point out objects that are near and those that are far. Then have your child use a pencil or crayon to draw a circle around the horse that is far and a dot next to the horse that is near. Invite your child to color the picture.

Near and Far
3-2-1 Learn, SV 9781419099281

Family Fun

Directions: Show your child a photo of your family. Ask your child to name the people and count them. Discuss activities that the family does together. Then have your child use a pencil or crayon to draw a picture of your family participating in his or her favorite activity.

Families Do Things Together
3-2-1 Learn, SV 9781419099281

Families

Directions: Invite your child to name a neighborhood friend. Help your child name and count the people in that friend's family. Discuss how that family is the same as and different from yours. Ask your child to tell which of the two families has more members. Then have your child look at the pictures and discuss how other families are the same and different. Have your child count the members in each family and use a pencil or crayon to circle the picture that shows more family members. Finally invite your child to color the pictures.

Families Are Different
3-2-1 Learn, SV 9781419099281

Happy Birthday

Directions: Discuss with your child the days of the year that your family celebrates. Show him or her pictures of those special celebrations. Then ask your child how he or she celebrates a birthday. Get a calendar and point out the day and month of your child's birthday. Then have your child use a pencil or crayon to draw candles on the cake to show how old he or she will be on the next birthday. Invite your child to color the cake.

Flying Flags

Directions: Show your child a map of North America. Point out that Mexico, the United States, and Canada are different countries, but they are neighbors. Show your child flags from the countries and explain that they are symbols. Then have your child identify each pattern and use a pencil or crayon to draw a line to the flag on the bottom that comes next.

Countries and Their Flags
3-2-1 Learn, SV 9781419099281

Things We Need

Directions: Discuss with your child that people have basic needs, including a place to live, food, clothes, and ways to move around. Have your child identify the objects and why we need them. Then have your child name the shapes, use a pencil or crayon to trace them, and color the pictures.

People Have Needs
3-2-1 Learn, SV 9781419099281

I Want....

Directions: On a trip to the grocery store, discuss with your child the foods that your family needs and why. Point out foods that are nice to have but that are not necessary for good health. Explain that these are the kinds of foods that people sometimes want. Help your child identify other examples of needs and wants. Then have your child use a pencil or crayon to cross out each object that is a want and color the object that is a need in each box.

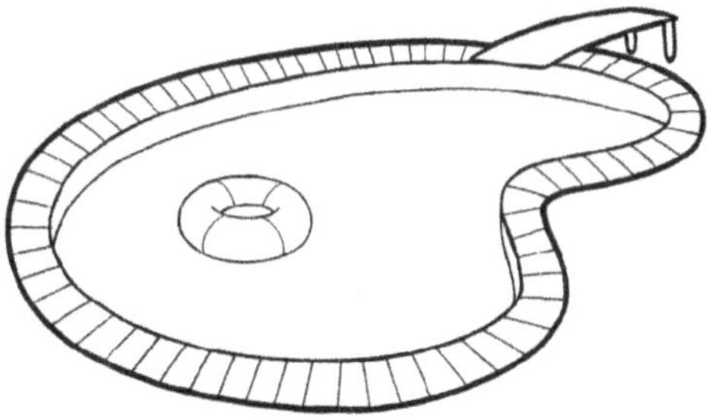

Money in the Bank

Directions: Show your child a penny, nickel, dime, and quarter. Ask your child to compare the sizes and colors of the coins. Then have your child color the two coins in each bank that are the same.

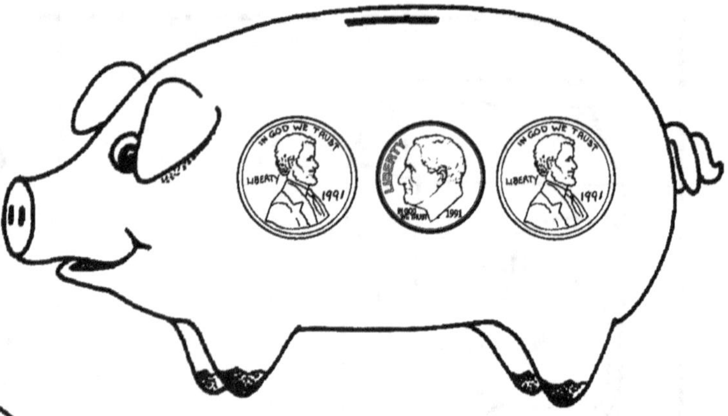

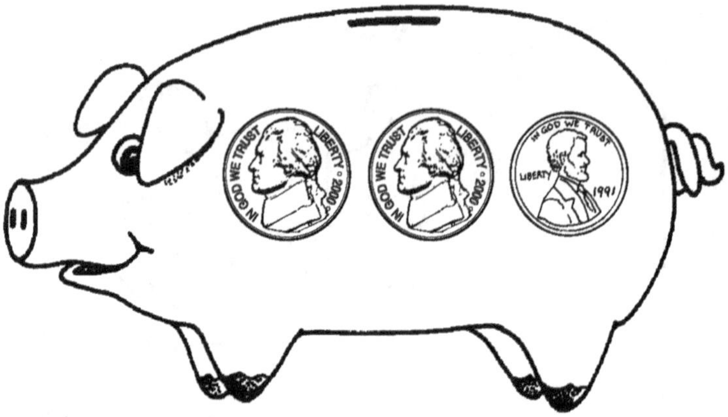

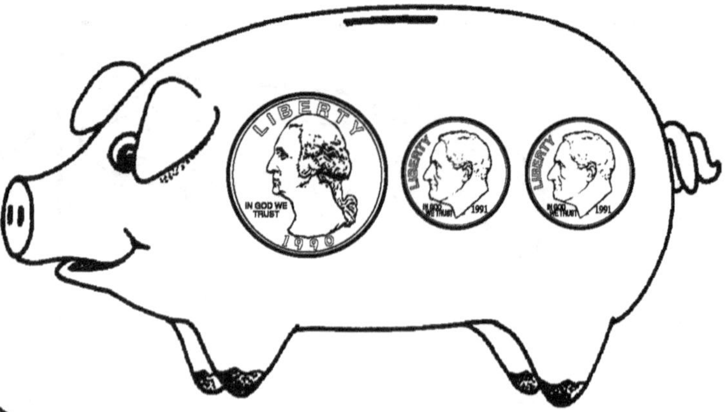

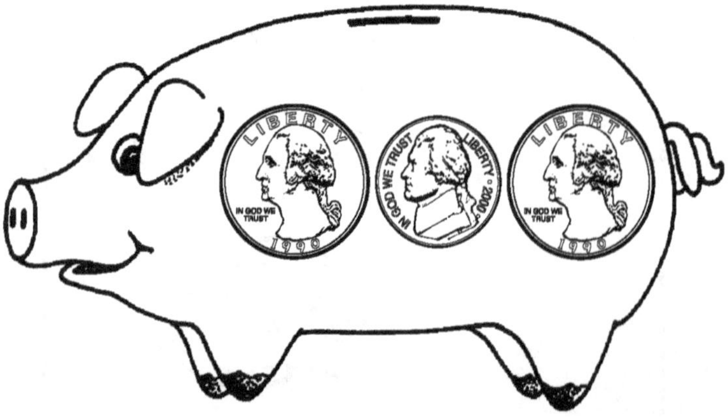

Coins
3-2-1 Learn, SV 9781419099281

Let's Go Shopping

Directions: Write price tags from one to ten cents for several toys. Invite your child to count out pennies to show the amount on each price tag. Then have your child color the pennies to show the amount on each tag.

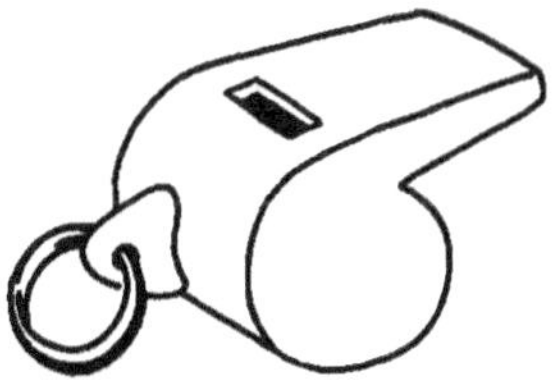

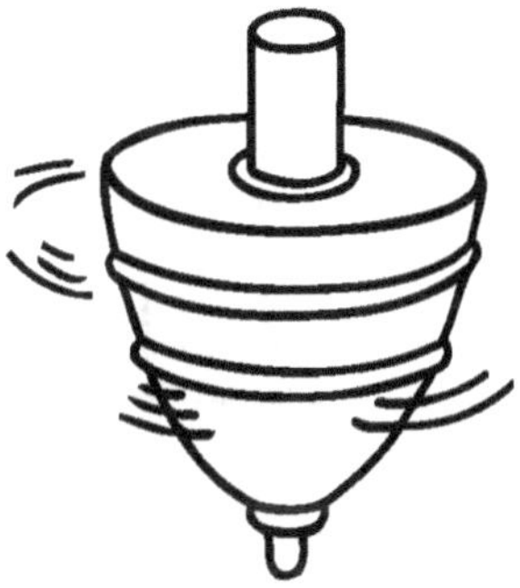

Toy	Price Tag	Pennies
(whistle)	3¢	(6 pennies)
(spinning top)	2¢	(6 pennies)
(pull-toy mouse)	5¢	(6 pennies)
(robot)	6¢	(6 pennies)

Count Pennies
3-2-1 Learn, SV 9781419099281

Who Keeps Us Safe?

Directions: While out in the community, point out to your child the people who keep everyone safe. Discuss the jobs they do and the tools they use. Then have your child color the people who keep everyone safe.

People in the Community
3-2-1 Learn, SV 9781419099281

Tooling Along

Directions: Discuss a job that a family member has and the tools the person uses. Then have your child identify the job that the picture in each row shows. Have your child use a pencil or crayon to cross out the tool that the person would not use. Invite your child to color the other pictures.

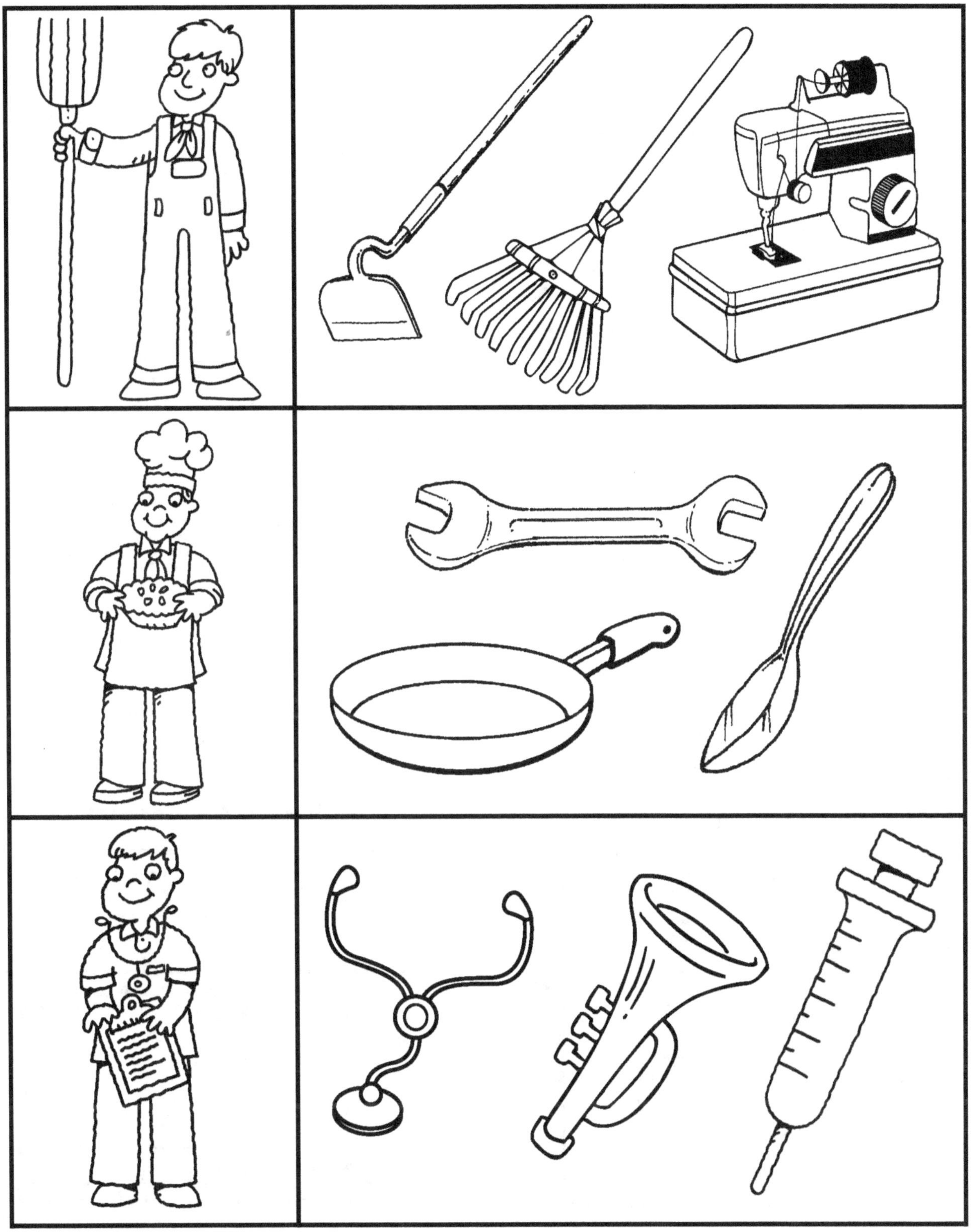

Tools People Use
3-2-1 Learn, SV 9781419099281

Shopping in the Stores

Directions: While shopping with your child, point out the different stores and the goods sold in each one. Then read the name of each store to your child. Have your child use a pencil or crayon to draw a picture of something he or she could buy in each store. Invite your child to color the pictures.

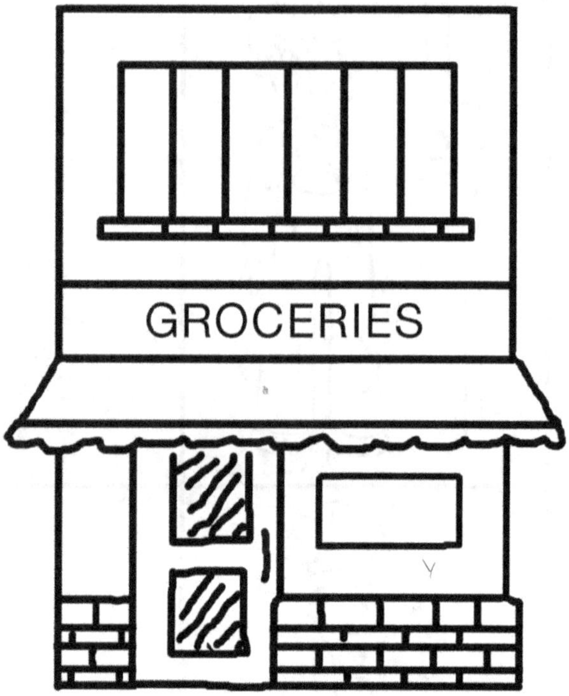

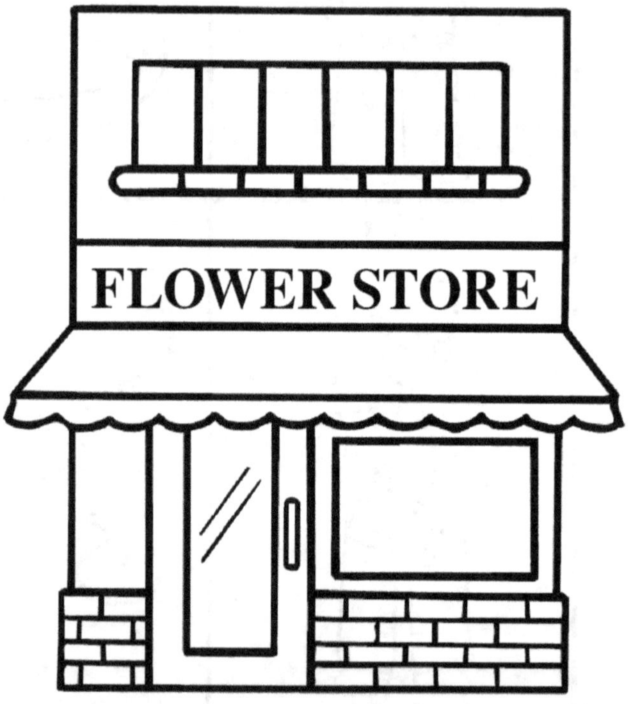

116

Stores in the Community
3-2-1 Learn, SV 9781419099281

Around Town

Directions: While out in the community, point out to your child that there are places to work and places to live. Help your child identify examples of each. Then have your child color the neighborhood picture. Have him or her use a pencil or crayon to circle the places where people live. Have your child draw a line under the places where people work.

Places to Work and Live
3-2-1 Learn, SV 9781419099281

Land and Water

Directions: Show your child a map of North America and explain its purpose. Point out the countries of Canada, the United States, and Mexico on the map. Explain the colors representing water and land and have your child identify these areas on the map. Then have your child use a blue crayon to color the water and a green crayon to color the land.

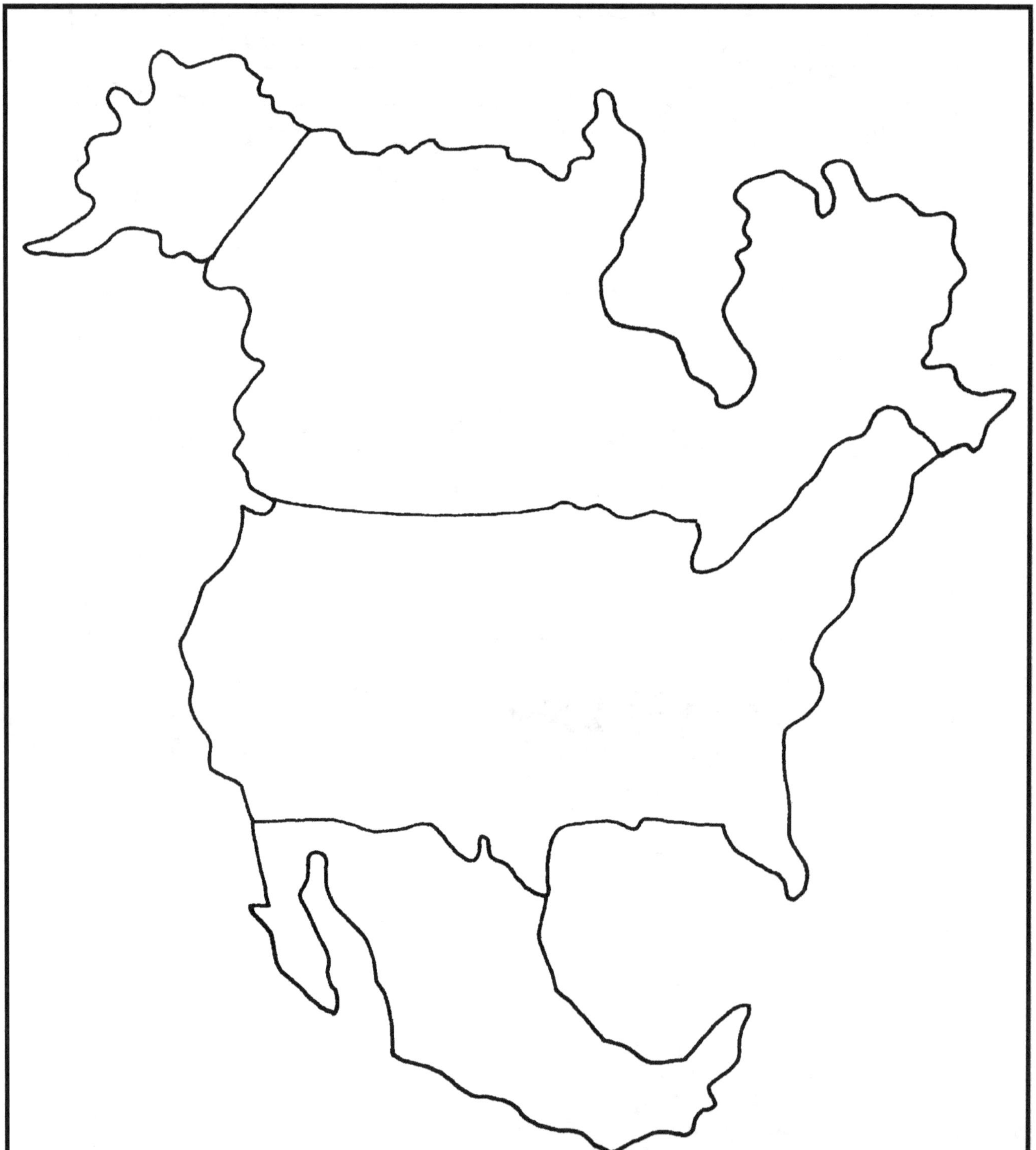

Visit a Zoo

Directions: Show your child a simple map and discuss its features and symbols. Then ask your child to look at the map of the zoo. Discuss how the two maps are alike and different. Point out that the animal faces below the map are symbols that match to the map. Have your child use a pencil or crayon to draw lines to show the path one family follows on their zoo trip.

Use a Map
3-2-1 Learn, SV 9781419099281

Follow the Rules

Directions: Talk with your child about rules the family has, including bedtime and eating. Then talk about safety rules in the community. Ask your child to color the pictures and explain the rule shown in each. Have your child use a pencil or crayon to trace the box around the pictures that show safety rules.

Seeing Signs

Directions: Point out signs around your community to your child and discuss their meaning.
Then have your child identify the signs, use a pencil or crayon to trace the outlines, and color them.

Good Citizens

Directions: Explain to your child what a citizen is and ways that people can be good citizens. Then have your child color the person in each scene who is being a good citizen and explain why.

Where Do I Work?

Directions: Show your child a picture of a man fishing. Discuss that people who live near water can have a job catching fish. Then have your child identify the job each person does and use a pencil or crayon to draw a line to a place where the person would work.

Where People Work
3-2-1 Learn, SV 9781419099281

Different Kinds of Jobs

Directions: While out in the community with your child, point out people who sell goods, provide a service, and make or grow something. Discuss how these jobs are alike and different. Then have your child use a pencil or crayon to circle the person who sells things, draw a line under the person who provides a service, and write an **X** next to the place where something is grown. Invite your child to color the pictures.

3-2-1 Learn, SV 9781419099281

Air, Land, or Water

Directions: Tell your child that people can travel in the air, on the land, or in the water. Then have your child identify the forms of transportation in each row and color the two that can be found in the same place.

Transportation
3-2-1 Learn, SV 9781419099281

On the Road Again

Directions: While driving or riding in a vehicle with your child, discuss why people make roads. Then have your child lead the mail truck to the post office by using a pencil or crayon to draw a line on the road.

Roads
3-2-1 Learn, SV 9781419099281

Get the News

Directions: Take a walk through the house with your child and look for machines that people can use to learn about what is happening in the community. Then have your child color the pictures that show the machines people can use to get information.

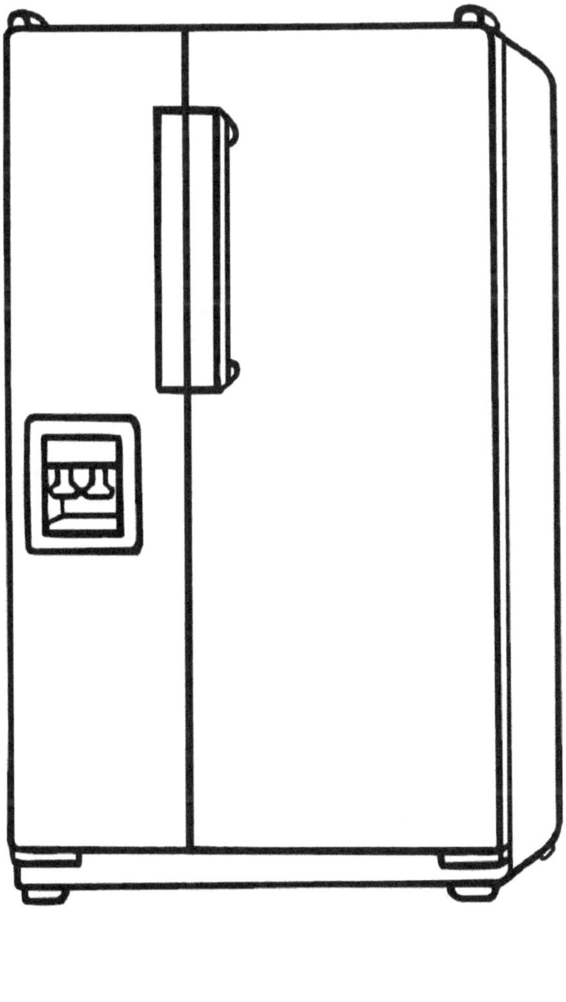

Then and Now

Directions: Light a candle and tell your child that people long ago lit candles so they could read at night. Ask your child what people use today to see at night. Then help your child identify the pictures on the left and their use in the past. Have your child use a pencil or crayon to draw a line to match the object from the past with the one that is used today. Invite your child to color the pictures.

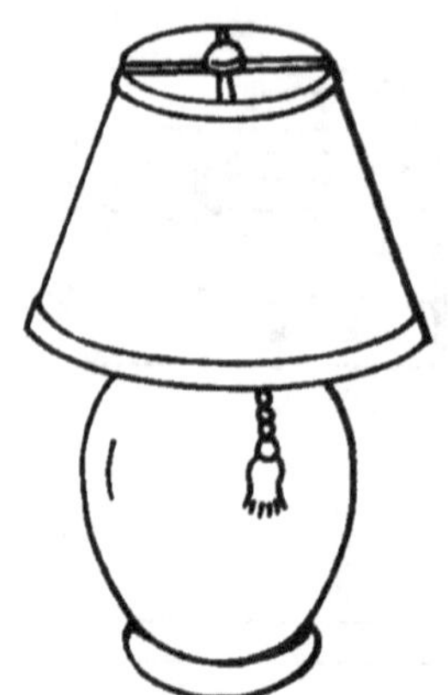

Past and Present
3-2-1 Learn, SV 9781419099281